# the social media SALES revolution

The New Rules for Finding Customers,
Building Relationships, and
Closing More Sales Through
Online Networking

## LANDY CHASE
## KEVIN KNEBL

New York   Chicago   San Francisco   Lisbon   London   Madrid   Mexico City
Milan   New Delhi   San Juan   Seoul   Singapore   Sydney   Toronto

The *McGraw·Hill* Companies

1 2 3 4 5 6 7 8 9 10 11 12 13 14 15  QFR/QFR  1 6 5 4 3 2 1

ISBN   978-0-07-176850-4
MHID       0-07-176850-5

e-ISBN  978-0-07-177455-0
e-MHID     0-07-177455-6

This publication is designed to provide accurate and authoritative information in regard to the subject matter covered. It is sold with the understanding that neither the author nor the publisher is engaged in rendering legal, accounting, securities trading, or other professional services. If legal advice or other expert assistance is required, the services of a competent professional person should be sought.

—*From a Declaration of Principles Jointly Adopted by a Committee of the American Bar Association and a Committee of Publishers and Associations*

**Library of Congress Cataloging-in-Publication Data**

Chase, Landy.
    The social media sales revolution : the new rules for finding customers, building relationships, and closing more sales through online networking / by Landy Chase and Keven Knebl. — 1st ed.
        p.    cm.
    Includes index.
    ISBN: 978-0-07-176850-4 (alk. paper)
    1. Selling.    2. Social media—Marketing.    I. Knebl, Kevin.    II. Title.
    HF5438.25.C479   2011
    658.8'72—dc22                                                2011009173

McGraw-Hill books are available at special quantity discounts to use as premiums and sales promotions or for use in corporate training programs. To contact a representative, please e-mail us at bulksales@mcgraw-hill.com.

This book is printed on acid-free paper.

*To my three wonderful children, who in their respective ways remind me daily of the success that their mother and I had in being parents. Nothing that I accomplish in my life will ever give me greater satisfaction; each of them is a treasure that this world is fortunate to have received.*
—Landy Chase

*To my beautiful wife, Karin, and our three amazing children, Anja, Tristan, and Calais, whose patience and encouragement I greatly appreciate while I travel and pursue my passion. I couldn't have a more supportive family, and I love them with all my heart.*
—Kevin Knebl

# CONTENTS

CHAPTER 4

**THE ROLE OF FACEBOOK IN
BUSINESS DEVELOPMENT**

CHAPTER 5

**BLOGGING IS EASIER THAN YOU THINK**

CHAPTER 6

**ATTRACTING ATTENTION TO YOUR
ONLINE PRESENCE**

CHAPTER 7

**HOW TO COMMUNICATE WITH PROSPECTS
ONLINE AND OFFLINE**

CHAPTER 8

**EFFECTIVE TIME MANAGEMENT**

CONTENTS

# PREFACE

It is seven thirty in the morning—in this case, a Friday morning—and Thomas, a business-to-business (B2B) sales professional for a technology company, is making final preparations for his weekly marketing effort. Like most high-achieving salespeople, Thomas is a creature of habit. Thus, Thomas always does his marketing work on Friday mornings. And, since Thomas is a salesperson, his "marketing work" this morning is, as it has always been, a telephone-prospecting session.

Thomas is the quintessential selling machine. He has a work ethic that is without peer. Colleagues admiringly refer to him as "Thomas the Sales Engine," a play on the fictional anthropomorphic steam locomotive in the Railway Series books. He is a planner, and he is disciplined. He comes into the office at the same time each day. He does the same activities at the same time each and every week. His goal today, as it has been every

PREFACE

Friday morning for hundreds of past Friday mornings, is to set four appointments.

Thomas is also well educated. He has attended numerous training seminars on effective prospecting techniques during his career. (In fact, in years past, he has attended traditional prospecting workshops given by both of the authors of this book.) He has also read extensively on the subject. Like most top sales pros, he is always looking for an edge—and, historically, he has always found what he is looking for.

Thomas's education and skill level are reflected in everything that he says on the telephone. By traditional standards, Thomas is as good at this type of work as anyone in the selling profession. He has all of the key attributes that make an outstanding cold caller successful. He is motivated. He is focused. He is articulate without being canned or slick. His approach with gatekeepers is polite and polished. His pitch to decision makers is also highly refined and spot-on in its effectiveness.

He is so good, in fact, that if he can just get a qualified decision maker on the telephone for 15 or 20 seconds, he can persuade many of them to grant him an appointment before the call is concluded.

Unfortunately for Thomas, therein lies the problem.

You see, over the past few years, Thomas has seen an alarming drop in the number of appointments that he is able to set each week. In fact, as recently as three years ago, Thomas didn't need to make 50 calls every Friday morning. He made just 25, because he almost always reached his four-appointment goal with this level of effort. Then, about three years ago, over the space of just a few months, he saw a sudden and significant drop in appointment results.

What concerned Thomas the most at the time was the fact that this drop was not the result of a change in his tried-and-true telephone techniques. Yet, without anything changing on his end, his success rate had taken a significant turn for the worse.

Unfortunately, Thomas reacted to this problem the way most salespeople would, and still do. Instead of examining the reasons behind the productivity drop, he simply did more of what he had always done successfully. He didn't work smarter; he worked harder—much harder. In this case, he doubled his calling effort without changing his fundamental skill set. He began making 50 calls every Friday morning, not 25. To his credit, he did make one significant technological adjustment: he acquired a contact-management software program and began managing his prospects on his laptop.

Three years ago, these adjustments paid the requisite dividends. Three years ago, he got back to his four-appointment goal each week, maintained his sales productivity and income level, and reinforced in his mind the idea that hard work will overcome any selling obstacle. Three years ago, Thomas's strategy worked.

Now Thomas has a bigger problem. The productivity issue has reared its ugly head again. This time around, however, it is not going to be defeated with old-fashioned hard work.

Thomas's strength, his trump card, has always been his ability to acquire new accounts through a consistent outbound marketing effort. But now, even Thomas's 50-call-a-week regimen isn't meeting his needs. In fact, he is having enormous difficulty in getting more than one prospect appointment a week, despite all his work. To complicate matters, Thomas cannot, as he did previously, increase the number of calls he makes, as there is no time for that in his schedule.

For Thomas, like many other salespeople, the economic down-turn has hit him where it hurts—right in his wallet. Through no fault of his own, he has lost nearly 20 percent of his customers, and most of the remaining 80 percent are buying less than they did in the "good old days." As we noted, Thomas is no longer able to replace the lost business through appointments generated from his weekly prospecting effort, and as a result, he is really feeling the heat.

Thomas has had several uncomfortable meetings with his sales manager in recent months. All of them have focused on one topic: his continued drop in sales performance. Each time, his man-ager, predictably, encourages him to work harder. The manager is a good leader, but he cannot provide what Thomas desperately needs, which is a solution to the revenue problem. Thomas is at the end of his rope. He is stressed, and he is frustrated. He knows that he has to do *something*, but for the first time in his career, he does not know what that "something" can be.

Thomas is out of ideas, but he is not stupid, he is not pas-sive, and he is not a quitter. He does something that he has not done in a very long time: he examines his marketing methods, his assumptions about what works in sales, and what is different about the marketplace. He opens up his mind. He takes a step back from the day-to-day struggle that his career has been of late, and he looks at what has changed in his world. He examines the steps in his weekly prospecting effort, and once he does that, it does not take him long to identify the root cause of the problem.

Thomas realizes that buyers are no longer reachable on their telephones, because the telephone is no longer their primary communication tool. Instead, they are doing most of their com-municating on the Internet. He realizes that his marketing efforts are going to have to adapt to this fundamental and irreversible change. He also realizes that social media offer him a huge opportunity to communicate with his customers and prospects in ways that he has never done before. It is at this point that Thomas makes the decision to purchase this book.

Your authors are here to help you—and we are exceptionally qualified to do so. You should know that we both enjoyed successful careers as salespeople. Independent of each other, we both developed and grew successful businesses that focused for years on training sales teams to generate new revenue, before we became involved in social media. Today, we are both prominent in this new field, and this work is the product of our own experience, of proven and replicable methods that both of us employ on a daily basis. We have collaborated to deliver to you the ultimate sales professional's user guide—the one road map that you need to generate offline revenue from online marketing. Yes, everything we share here is field-tested—and it works! So turn the page. Join us now, and join *The Social Media Sales Revolution*.

Landy Chase
Kevin Knebl

# ACKNOWLEDGMENTS

## Landy Chase

This book was, for me, both a rewarding and a challenging project, written during a year of transition, change, and personal growth. Special thanks to

Betsy Padgett, Anna B. Padgett, Russell Powell, Johnny Hoover, Jenni Lanning, Jay Lucas, and Beth Lucas

My parents

David Meerman Scott, for his book *The New Rules of Marketing and PR*

My coauthor, Kevin Knebl, for his collaboration and for meeting all those deadlines

Patsy Stewart, for her advice and patience, and for going the extra mile

Ira Kaufman, for his creativity and brilliant mind

Regina Landry, for your continued hard work and loyalty

## Kevin Knebl

I had a wonderful time writing this book. It was an honor and a privilege to be able to coauthor this volume. Special thanks to

My good friend Chris Kauza, for his encouragement and his brilliant marketing mind

David Fein, for his example of what can be accomplished when you seek first to serve

Joseph Berkowitz and Stephanie Frerich at McGraw-Hill, for their invaluable assistance

My coauthor, Landy Chase, for being such a great collaborator and for his patience with my right-brain ways

My parents, Karl and Anne Knebl, for their support and encouragement

My wife, Karin, for her never-ending belief in me

CHAPTER **1**

# GAME CHANGERS

## The Six Rules of the Social Media Sales Revolution

Before we get into the details of the Social Media Sales Revolution, let's turn the clock back a little and take a look at how we got here.

## Landy's Story

In 1985, Landy started his first job as a business-to-business (B2B) salesperson. The company that hired him was a bootstrap start-up with a small amount of capital. However, it was an opportunity in outside sales, which was beneficial for a young person with no sales experience. Landy was a good fit for the company, and vice versa. He jumped at the opportunity, partly because the company was willing to give him a chance, even without a proven track record, and partly because it was introducing a new idea that it seemed to him would change the business world forever.

Believe it or not, back in those days people at work actually received incoming messages from outside callers on slips of paper! It worked like this: the office secretary would take the call (that's right—this was before the term *executive assistant* came into favor), write down the caller's information on a small preprinted slip, and place the message from the caller in the recipient's inbox slot on the secretary's desk. There was an individual slot for each employee for this purpose. The recipient would then come to the secretary's desk, check his or her slot, retrieve any messages taken by the secretary, read them, and return phone calls. It was just like going out to your mailbox at home and checking for mail, only it happened at the office.

This company's new service was called *recorded message retrieval*, and it eliminated the need for written messages. When a client signed up for this service, he would forward her phone number to the company. A bank of telephone operators at computer terminals took the clients' incoming calls. While the operator was handling the call, the conversation between the operator and the caller was recorded! When the client wanted to check her messages, she would call into her mailbox and listen, as a third party, to the recorded conversations that had taken place between the operator and the callers. This was 1985, though, so it seemed like amazing technology.

Landy hit the streets hard, presenting this exciting new service to business owners around Dallas, Texas. Nobody had ever seen anything like it—and Landy's enthusiasm for the service was contagious. Within six months, he was, at the ripe old age of 23, the company's number two salesperson in the United States. Then, one Friday afternoon, the company announced that it had run out of funding, and Landy, having been previously tipped off about the firm's dire financial straits, accepted a better job with a publicly held company in the office-products business the following Monday morning.

You know the technology, of course; you use it every day. It is called voice mail.

There have been many other changes in business communication over the past 25 years, and these, in turn, have been driven mostly by new technology. For example, when Landy was selling "recorded message retrieval" in 1985, salespeople did not use personal computers. (He bought his first PC, a desktop IBM XT, in 1987. It came with a dot-matrix printer.) We did not have laser printers. We did not have cell phones or PDAs. We usually did not have fax machines. Over the years, as each of these products arrived, the technology came in the form of easily manageable gadgets that one could learn to use without difficulty. Then came the Internet.

## The Ultimate Game Changer

The Internet is the greatest communication tool of all time. For B2B sales people, it is also the ultimate game changer. Past technological changes have all been improvements like voice mail, which were easily adaptable to the existing landscape, whereas the Internet is not. Over the past 15 years, it has completely taken over the way in which people get and exchange information. Over the past five, it has completely taken over the way in which people socialize with one another.

And now—right now, as this book is being written—social networking is taking over B2B communication. Like it or not, social networking sites are completely, and permanently, redefining the way salespeople find new customers.

The good news is that if you learn to harness the power of this new technology, it can grow your sales like nothing that has come before. The bad news? If you don't adapt quickly to this fundamentally new way of building relationships, you will, in all likelihood, find yourself locked out of the selling profession. The moment has come to learn and adapt. Selling is undergoing a revolution, and the times they are a-changin'.

## The Six Rules

The Internet has created six fundamental shifts in the B2B marketplace that are driving the future of the selling profession. They require all of us who wish to sell successfully in the new marketplace to accept these changes, recognize the inherent opportunities that they offer, and become educated in the new skills needed to acquire new customers.

In this chapter, our aim is to convince you to embrace the new fundamental rules for salespeople that together make up the Social Media Sales Revolution. You will find some of your most fundamental beliefs regarding how you should be doing your job challenged. You may even find yourself questioning what you should be doing for a living. If, at the end of this chapter, you are in agreement with these six points, then you will find the rest of the book to be a career-changing educational experience. And you will be ready to get on board and join the revolution.

## Rule 1: Abandon Traditional Prospecting

As career sales trainers and speakers who have specialized in teaching traditional prospecting skills to salespeople for more than 20 years, we obviously wish that those skills would remain relevant forever. Unfortunately, they are rapidly on their way to becoming irrelevant. Traditional prospecting is fast becoming obsolete as a selling skill. This is happening because the telephone is increasingly becoming obsolete as a business communication tool. The vast majority of B2B correspondence now occurs through e-mail, simply because online communication is vastly superior to the telephone as a means of sharing information. Here are just a few examples of the advantages that e-mail offers:

- The ability to communicate with as many people, simultaneously, as one wishes
- The ability to communicate 24/7
- The ability to talk to another person without actually talking to him
- The ability to think through a conversation with a seller without the rapid-fire back-and-forth of a live conversation
- The ability to respond at one's leisure during the course of an ongoing conversation
- The ability to communicate without interruption
- The ability to communicate in total privacy
- The ability to send documents within a conversation
- The ability to ignore communication without hanging up on the other party

- The ability to delete unimportant or unwanted communications immediately
- The ability to review a complete, written record of past conversations, which eliminates the need for taking notes or trying to remember details
- The ability to say no without the stress of having to explain one's reasons to a live person

This shift away from traditional prospecting is both bad and good news for the sales profession. The bad news, as we outlined earlier, is that it is almost impossible to reach prospects on the telephone. When was the last time that you had consistent success in talking to a "live" prospect when making prospecting calls? The problem you face has little to do with your skill level in prospecting. It has everything to do with the fact that decision makers no longer have to tolerate the interruption inherent in answering the telephone. Most of their important business correspondence comes in through their in-box, not the phone line.

Additionally, voice mail eliminates any worry about a missed call; the information can be stored there and retrieved at the recipient's convenience. Today, people can, and do, ignore the occasional ring of the telephone with little risk of penalty. Whether you are a salesperson, an employee, or a relative, whenever you call someone at her place of business, your success rate in reaching her is equally poor—and it is only going to get worse.

This is why our friend in the Preface, Thomas the Sales Engine, narrowly escaped failure in spite of his work ethic. Thomas believed, based on past experience, that he could succeed solely through his labor and his drive. He responded to the communication shift with more effort, and for a time, he was successful. He made the most cold calls of anyone in the office, he got a handful of marginally qualified appointments, and he congratulated himself on a job well done. He did this because he did not know of any other way to succeed. He utilized the least productive form of marketing available to him, partly because it was all that he knew, but also because it was, for a long time, all that he had chosen to learn. The near-tragedy of Thomas was that eventually, he was good at nothing more than performing a primitive, outdated, and unproductive marketing technique that had no place in the new selling environment. Thomas, like every other salesperson, depends on new selling opportunities to grow his customer base. The day will soon come, if it is not upon us already, when all salespeople will be facing this same inability to reach new customers through traditional means. The choice they will all face is simple: join the Social Media Sales Revolution or look for another job in another line of work.

The wonderful news is that the online world is an infinitely superior environment for developing new relationships with prospective buyers, because the same benefits of online correspondence outlined for them also apply to salespeople. However, as we will discuss in more detail later in this book, you can forget about "cold calling" prospects on the Internet, too. What you will need is a completely different mindset regarding what works, and what doesn't, when developing new business.

## Rule 2: Become a Marketer First and a Seller Second

Within the sales profession, it has always been universally assumed that the most productive salespeople are those who have the most polished selling skills. In the selling revolution, that sacred-cow assumption is absolutely, fundamentally wrong. To prove it, let's begin with the following definitions of *marketing* and *selling*.

Our definition of marketing: *marketing* means participating in activities that create opportunities to sell. In other words, anything that generates a sales opportunity—be it advertising, networking, mailings, e-mail blasts, or, yes, good old-fashioned prospecting—is a form of marketing, because all these activities generate opportunities to sell.

How do we then define selling? How about this: *selling* is what you get to do if your marketing *works*. The point? As a salesperson, your success depends not nearly so much on being skilled at *selling* as it does on being skilled at *marketing*. Yes, you may have superb selling skills. You may have mastered every step in the selling cycle—opening meetings properly, conducting the needs analysis, presenting recommendations, negotiating, and closing. Well, so what? If you aren't getting opportunities to execute these steps consistently with qualified buyers, what good are those skills doing you? You may end up as a highly skilled failure.

On the other hand, if you are good at marketing—if you are skilled at consistently creating opportunities for qualified buyers to meet with you—you might be mediocre at selling and still enjoy great success as a salesperson. If you have superb selling skills too, well, you can own the world.

It's fairly simple: marketing skills are the key to sales success, and therein lies the problem. The sales profession, in its present state, has a huge productivity issue, because for most salespeople, traditional prospecting *is* marketing—it is all they know. The fact of the matter is that, no matter how skilled you are at prospecting, no matter what method you use, you cannot get around the fact that you are still bugging strangers for appointments—with predictable results.

Prospecting is not the only form of marketing that has this inherent liability; in fact, *all* traditional marketing methods do.

In his landmark bestseller on the subject of social media marketing, *The New Rules of Marketing and PR*, David Meerman Scott refers to traditional advertising as "product-focused one-way spin." As he points out, the vast majority of advertising efforts, irrespective of the delivery method, are conceived, created, and delivered for the sole purpose of bugging the recipient. When your prospect is watching TV, his chosen program is periodically stopped to allow commercials. When your prospect listens to the radio, he is forced to sit through all manner of product pitches to get back to listening to music. When your prospect picks up a magazine, he must flip through page after page of advertising clutter to get to the article that he wants to read. And, when your prospect receives a cold call from a salesperson, his work is being interrupted to respond to an inquiry that is neither needed nor expected. Traditional marketing, in all its forms, is therefore an unwelcome intrusion. It is uninvited, unvalued, and, at best, marginally effective.

This is the fundamental problem that is limiting the effectiveness of all traditional marketing, including prospecting: it is not welcome. Until the advent of the Internet, traditional "push" methods were all that were available to marketers. Until the explosion of social media marketing, traditional prospecting was the only marketing strategy that salespeople had.

That is no longer the case. No longer will you need to bug people to get their attention. Instead, you are going to learn to change their behavior. You are going to be a person whose message is always valuable, and therefore always welcome.

One of the reasons why understanding and utilizing effective social media marketing skills is so important is that the online world really belongs to the customer. The social networking platforms are controlled by the people who use them. These information and conversation streams are never-ending. The old days of just blasting your information out and hoping that something will stick somewhere are over. People aren't just sitting passively and listening to pitches; they're deciding how, when, and what they want to listen to regarding their messages and then interacting with them. Resisting this change is like trying to fight nature. You will lose.

There is a natural flow to things, and this is the way in which communication is going. The old rules no longer apply. Learning how to maximize your social media efforts is about understanding how people gather and process information in this always-on environment and then using this information to your advantage. The goal of marketing has always been to compel people to take action. What's different now is that the tools are changing.

In today's world, technology has forever changed the way business gets done. However, the name of the game in marketing remains the same: efficiency. For salespeople, this means one thing: generating high-quality sales leads via an effective, well-designed online marketing strategy.

## Rule 3: Build Your Sphere of Influence

When Landy left the corporate world and started his own business in 1993, his initial market focus was on providing sales force training and consulting services to companies within the local community, which at that time was Cincinnati, Ohio. Recognizing that networking within the business community was an important component of finding new clients, he immediately joined the local chamber of commerce.

During the years that Landy was as a member there, the Greater Cincinnati Chamber of Commerce proved to be an excellent investment of both time and money for his small business. Like most chambers, this one provided ample opportunities for meeting new people through networking events. The basic format for networking when you work with any number of chamber of commerce branches is always the same: the event is a social get-together with an educational component, usually in the form of a local speaker. In addition to developing new clients through the chamber, Landy also made a lot of great friends that way, many of whom he still stays in touch with—online, of course.

This regular participation in chamber networking events provided Landy with an excellent education in how to develop new clients through in-person networking—by gradually building a sphere of influence. From that experience, three key tenets of business social networking became clear:

1. Soliciting business at networking events is a big no-no. You are there to socialize, not to sell. If you develop a reputation for pitching your services at a networking event, you will be quickly blacklisted.

2. Very little of the business that you generate from networking comes directly from people that you meet through networking.
3. Most of the business that finds you comes in the form of referrals—strangers to whom you are recommended by a mutual contact.

Networking in this way—the old-fashioned way—is fun, and if you stick with it, it is productive. However, it is labor-intensive, and it has some significant limitations. For one thing, you cannot meet someone in person and know, immediately, whom you mutually have in common. In this environment, that information, if it comes up at all, does so by chance. It is also a long, arduous process because it requires you to build your sphere of influence through face-to-face interaction with one person at a time and then hope that some of the people you meet will refer you to people who can do business with you.

Social media networking works in exactly the same way, and it also follows the same three rules—especially the one about not directly soliciting business. You will never accomplish anything online by treating the social networking community as a target for cold calls. However, unlike traditional networking, online networking puts real marketing power in your hands. It puts you in control of making connections with potential buyers quickly, and it amplifies your opportunities exponentially. To cite just a few examples, through social media

- You are continually being presented with new people that you may know, so you do not have to go looking for them.

- Every person who is presented to you for this purpose knows someone that you also know, which is why that person is being presented to you.
- The system tells you exactly who your mutual contacts are.

You can see where this is going. When you always have something in common with every new contact in your market, you have an in that changes the playing field permanently. What is the point of bugging complete strangers when you have this kind of power? Your sphere of influence is no longer limited to those people that you know; it now includes all the people that your existing contacts know as well. When it comes to building relationships, your world—and your opportunity—just got much, much bigger.

The number of businesspeople who are actively participating in this area is exploding. To cite one example, at the writing of this book, LinkedIn, which is currently the primary social media marketing outlet for business professionals, has more than 90 million members.

In Landy's last book, *Competitive Selling*, he makes the point that if we apply the Pareto Principle, or the 80/20 rule, to your market or sales territory, 20 percent of your prospects represent 80 percent of your potential business growth. The vast majority of this top 20 percent group of key people are the movers and shakers within any industry—and thus are heavily represented on social media websites like LinkedIn.

The message? Ignore this group of people at your own peril. And if you're not going where the action is online, then you are, in fact, ignoring this group.

Remember that as you participate online, you're not just finding out information about people, you're interacting with them. The more interaction you have with people online, the more you'll be building relationships through your computer. Finally, building your sphere of influence online will give you access to a much larger number of people than you could ever develop a relationship with solely offline.

## Rule 4: Become a Value Generator

In today's hypercompetitive business environment, buyers believe that they can get what you sell from any number of different vendors and be reasonably satisfied with the purchase. You, as a salesperson, probably disagree with them on this, and you may very well be right. However, it does not matter. The issue of accuracy is irrelevant here; the fact that *buyers believe it* is all that matters. Therefore, the marketplace views whatever product or service you actually sell as another commodity. Again, within a new dynamic, we find both a problem and an opportunity.

The problem you face here is that if you focus on trying to differentiate your offering based on features and benefits, the only way in which you are going to consistently win business is by lowering your price. In other words, the one benefit that you offer the marketplace is the ability to provide the same thing as everyone else for less money.

The opportunity here is that, in a business climate in which product differentiation is lacking, buyers have come to realize that good, useful advice is valuable—in fact, your potential customers value it more than they value anything else that you can offer as a salesperson. If the marketplace sees you as a qualified expert—if you are a source for timely, relevant information that your sphere of influence can find benefit in—then the marketplace will come to *you* to obtain that advice. Put another way, if you consistently provide people with good ideas for running a business better, they will buy from you primarily because they value your opinion. Yes, people can buy what you sell from someone else, but the risk of giving up your expertise overrides the benefit of changing vendors, even for a lower price.

The challenge that good salespeople have always had with this all-important "advisor" aspect of the job is the difficulty inherent in establishing one's expertise. In the past, this process took months, or even years, to accomplish because a salesperson first had to establish a face-to-face relationship with the buyer in order to provide this advice.

That has all changed with the advent of the Internet. As noted earlier, your buyers are doing most of their communicating online. Part of that communication involves seeking out information, and much of that information comes from people who have the industry experience and the skill base to provide it.

Salespeople who know how to place their expertise in front of a potential customer who is in need of such advice can obviously reap huge rewards in the online environment. Salespeople must therefore change the way they think when it comes to making contact with potential customers. Instead of working in an environment in which we push our message on potential prospects by cold calling, we must reverse the current. We must learn to pull prospects who are in need of good advice to us. This will happen not because we want them to hear our sales pitch but because they want our opinion. When they value our opinion, they will become our customers.

Thus, the Internet has become the source for exchanging information, and with this, it has become the primary delivery mechanism for dispensing advice. Your prospects no longer need to call someone to get useful ideas; the Web makes all the information in the world available in an instant. Instead of having a meeting with an outside vendor to discuss a need or a problem, your buyers can do research on their own, at their leisure, and in the privacy of their office. Instead of having to ask the vendor a question for clarification, your buyer can narrow down his online search with a few keystrokes. In these respects, the need to call in an advisor for business problems has been severely diminished.

So the salesperson of the future will be not a solicitor but a *value generator*, an individual who serves her online community as a dependable source of immediately usable, high-quality advice and ideas. The salesperson of the future is interested in people— all people, not just prospects. The focus here is on giving, not taking. Success is measured in terms of quantity of followers, not just quality. The greater the number of people who "know" the salesperson, the greater the number of leads that will surface for her. Salespeople understand that in a more and more transparent world, what goes around comes around, and that also applies to value. When you are always seeking to add value, more sales opportunities will open up for you and the people with whom you do business. And that's really what being a value generator is all about.

## Rule 5: Build Your Personal Brand

You have heard the old sales adage, "People buy from people they know." That is true, and it is one aspect of professional selling that has not changed, and will not in the future. However, in today's marketplace, the term *know* can mean many things, as there are different levels of "knowing." A better choice of words might be this: "People buy from people with whom they are familiar."

While we are at it, it would be worth a moment to consider *why* people like to buy from people with whom they are familiar. The reason is simple: in a world of choices, the more familiar you are to your prospective buyer, the less the perception of risk in doing business with you.

We noted earlier that buyers place a premium on useful advice. To take that idea a step further, it is important to note that advice from a known entity—specifically, a trusted authority—is of much greater interest, and is given much higher credence, than information from an unknown entity, because in the case of the unknown, the source of the expertise has not been validated. In other words, the recipient perceives the known-advisory source as being low risk based on positive experience with that advice provider in the past. This is the power of branding. It was true in the traditional marketing model, and it is a key point that carries over to the online one, as well. The logical conclusion is that salespeople need to become known entities to the prospects within their market.

This relationship between trust and risk also benefits you through having people vouch for you; the most common example is the testimonial letter. You already know how powerful a written endorsement is, but you also know that in the offline world, getting these written recommendations takes a considerable amount of work and effort. In the online world, getting ringing endorsements from customers is a snap. We will cover how to do this in depth in a later chapter.

It's important that you use one characteristic or another to distinguish yourself online. Whatever it is that makes you stand out, that is your brand, and in the online world, having a brand is a must. Remember that you are a marketer first and a salesperson second. As a marketer, you can, and must, distinguish yourself as a provider of consistently good advice. Social media marketing provides you with the power to build your reputation (your brand) as an expert within your field of business.

The primary value of establishing your personal brand is what is referred to in the advertising business as TOMA. TOMA, as you may already know, stands for *top of mind awareness*. Think of TOMA as your personal street cred. It represents the degree of significance with which you are regarded by those within your sphere of influence. In social media networking, TOMA (your degree of significance) is determined by two factors:

- The quality of the information (advice) that you provide to your sphere of influence
- The frequency with which you provide this information, which determines how often you are top of mind

The true sales pro will take TOMA to the next level, which is TOMATO. TOMATO stands for *top of mind awareness through others*. It's one thing to be at the forefront of people's minds and have them referring business to you. It's a whole other thing to have them telling others about you and referring you business without even having met you. If you create a strong personal brand and leverage social media, you will be amazed at how interconnected the world is and where opportunities come from.

Therefore, to build both street cred and familiarity, you must provide high-quality information to your sphere of influence, and you must do so on a regular basis. We will outline how to accomplish this with consistency and effectiveness later in the book.

## Rule 6: Work the Window

If you are like most successful salespeople, you have a genetic, built-in need for immediate gratification. That is also completely understandable. After all, you have sales numbers to generate. You have a quota to meet. You need new business—today!

If you are one of these people, and you wish to succeed in the selling revolution, you aren't going to like Rule 6. This one takes commitment and discipline. You must learn to think long term. You must learn to be patient. You must build your marketing strategy as a value generator within the context of how most purchase decisions are actually made.

In most B2B purchase decisions, the buying cycle follows this basic process:

Buyer has no need
↓
Buyer identifies a need
↓
Buyer chooses vendor; buyer makes purchase
↓
Need fulfilled; buyer again has no need

Branding is critical in B2B purchase decisions because the window of opportunity—when the buyer has a need—is a *temporary state*. It does not last. Buyers go from not having a need, to having a need and filling it, to not having a need again. The shut window opens, a decision is made, and then the window shuts again. This also means that, contrary to the popular misconception among many salespeople, purchase decisions are driven mostly by the efforts of the buyer to find a seller, not the other way around. Top salespeople bear out this point. If you spend a considerable amount of time, as we have, around different sales teams, you will notice that the top producers are consistently the ones that receive the most incoming leads. What most of their peers fail to understand is that the volume of leads to these top reps is not the result of luck, good fortune, or a hot territory. It materializes because the big hitters have established themselves, over time, as go-to people when buyers within their area of responsibility are in the window and have a need for what they sell.

In spite of this point, most marketing efforts ignore the role of the window. They are designed for the quick kill. They are created solely to pick up any immediate-need buyers while ignoring the timing factor, and with it, the remainder of the market.

To cite but one example, a business sector that never ceases to amaze us with its utter lack of understanding of this principle is car dealerships. You would expect car dealerships to be astute at marketing. In our opinion, they are anything but. Of course, these are the same people who place a 75-foot Godzilla in front of their place of business to attract buyers ("Look, honey, an inflated monster! I suddenly have an overwhelming urge to buy a new car"). We shouldn't find it surprising that, in spite of the fact that only 2 percent of the buying public is actively shopping for a car at any given time, most car dealers spend virtually their entire marketing budget on short-term advertising campaigns that focus exclusively on reaching that 2 percent. They measure the effectiveness of their marketing by how many people show up on their lot the day after the ads appear, and they ignore the need to build their brand with the other 98 percent of the market, most of whom will purchase a vehicle within the next five years.

The issue of timing is another problem that is inherent in traditional prospecting techniques. Cold-calling salespeople also fail to take the issue of timing into account when they are executing their marketing strategy. When a "push" marketing call is made, the salesperson is hoping to get lucky, to trip over a person who just happens to have a need for what the salesperson is selling at the moment that the contact is made. From a marketing standpoint, this is an exercise in futility because the timing factor is being ignored.

In most cases, we cannot control when a person is ready to buy. However, we can heavily influence which salespeople the buyer goes to when he is ready to buy, because when your buyer has a need, he will look for the option with the least risk. If a known entity is available, he will approach that entity first to fill that need. This is what branding is all about.

The great game-changing aspect of social media marketing is that it exponentially reduces the time required to become a go-to person within your market and to be consistently present when the window opens. Your job is to work the window.

## Let's Get Started

If you've read this far, you can see the blueprint for your own very bright future. By connecting with mutual contacts online—properly, as we will discuss later—you have the ability to add them to your sphere of influence. You aren't going to "sell" to them; on the contrary, you are going to become their favorite value generator and pull them to you. You are going to build your personal brand. You are going to establish TOMA. You are going to work the window. And when the window opens, your contacts are going to invite you to sell to them, because people like to buy from people with whom they are familiar. When you accomplish all of this, you will have become an active participant in the Social Media Sales Revolution.

## Summary

The bottom line is that the skills that made you successful in developing new business opportunities have fundamentally changed. Your success today is dependent on your skill as a marketer more than on your skill as a salesperson. Your mindset as a marketer needs to change focus from finding someone to whom you can sell to finding someone that you can help. As the great Zig Ziglar said, "You will always get what you want, if you help enough people get what they want." Social media is the perfect platform for helping enough people to get what they want. And by doing so, you will get what you want, too.

# CHAPTER 2

# LOCK IN SALES WITH LinkedIn

## The Gold Standard of Business Social Networking Sites

L inkedIn is the world's standard for online business networking. It has more than 110 million members as this is being written, and it is growing by the minute. Sales professionals, rejoice: the average member is 43 years old and earns $107,000 per year. Not a bad business demographic! In this chapter, we will be taking an in-depth look at what this social media platform can do for you.

## LinkedIn: The Basics

As the world is getting smaller, the number of professionals who are using LinkedIn is getting bigger. LinkedIn is generally thought of as a social networking platform, but in reality it is the world's best business networking database. LinkedIn is not "social" in the sense of posting personal, non-work-related information. It is all about business. It is a database in the most literal, and powerful, meaning of the word. You can strategically search through LinkedIn and identify people and organizations that you want to sell to, create alliances with, hire, refer business to, network with, and add value to as a professional.

All the Fortune 500 companies use LinkedIn as a business tool. For the professional salesperson, having a working knowledge of LinkedIn has gone from being a benefit to being a necessity in a relatively short period of time. Unfortunately, as of this writing, the vast majority of salespeople are still of the mindset that this social media outlet is something that is nice to participate in but is by no means required. We are going to work hard in this chapter to change the belief of any readers who still feel that way. By using LinkedIn properly, you can do more than just network. You can learn extremely important things about other professionals, and you can achieve profound results in your offline sales efforts.

Having a robust LinkedIn account that properly portrays you as the consummate sales professional that you are is a very important tool in establishing your online credibility. Moreover, as you will see, it is just as important to your prospects. You will want to make sure that your credentials, experience, and interests all add up to form a complete picture of who you are, what you do, and, especially, the value proposition that you, personally, bring to the marketplace. This point applies equally to your prospects; by looking at a prospect's LinkedIn profile, you can gather a lot of useful information about him—information that can be useful in making connections and, eventually, initiating sales opportunities.

If you're not using LinkedIn to its full capabilities, rest assured that you're leaving a lot of money on the table. We can guarantee that your competitors either are already on the LinkedIn band-wagon or are getting onto it. Prospective clients are busier than ever, and they are spending more and more time online. If they can look at your LinkedIn profile and determine that you are credible and that you represent yourself and your organization well, that saves them a lot of time in performing their due diligence. The reverse of this scenario is equally valuable to you as a sales professional; you can do market research, monitor the competition, and find viable business rapidly.

Every sharp businessperson that we know uses LinkedIn to learn more about the people and companies that she is thinking about doing business with, which means that if you're not there, you're not as relevant as you think you are. Sorry to be so blunt, but that's the way it is. By not having a presence on LinkedIn, a salesperson is telling the top guns in the business world that he doesn't *want* to do business with them. How do you dance with someone if you aren't actually at the dance? You don't. So read on, learn how to do The LinkedIn Shuffle, and avoid being a sales wallflower.

# The Changing Face of the Internet

You already know that technology is evolving at a breakneck pace. Simply performing a search with Google is a twentieth-century technique—and we have already entered the second decade of the twenty-first century. Of course, someone can and hopefully still will Google your name or the name of your company, but here's a market dynamic that you should be aware of: more sophisticated businesspeople are often going to LinkedIn even before they go to Google to do their due diligence. They are migrating over, in greater and greater numbers, as this book is being written. That trend is only going to accelerate.

LinkedIn was formed in 2002 by several Silicon Valley software executives and venture capital firms. It was created out of a desire to combine the concept of the traditional offline Rolodex with online software that allows not only storage for contacts, but also the ability to view the hidden connections between business professionals.

We could write an entire book just on the basics of LinkedIn and how to use it most effectively, but there are other resources that address that topic. We will assume that you already have a LinkedIn profile, but that, like more than 90 percent of salespeople, you haven't done much beyond creating it. (If you do not yet have a LinkedIn account, put this book down right now, create one, and then come back to this page.) With that in mind, this chapter is divided into seven sections that correspond to some of the sections on LinkedIn: "Your Profile," "Managing Contacts," "Advanced Search," "Companies," "Groups," "Answers," and "Events." The nature of social networking is such that there are always going to be new and enhanced tools added to sites like LinkedIn, but by familiarizing yourself with the core tools that are available right now, you can maximize the site's benefits with the least amount of time and effort. Beyond that, keeping up with updates to LinkedIn will fall in step with your work habits, as we will mention here and then cover in depth in a subsequent chapter. To gain the most benefit from this chapter, we recommend that you log on to your LinkedIn account at this point and follow along from here.

# Your LinkedIn Profile

As a sales professional who uses LinkedIn effectively, you have the opportunity to position yourself in the marketplace as the credible businessperson that you are. As we mentioned before, having a polished, complete LinkedIn profile is an absolute requirement; it provides you with a platform that you can use to market your expertise. It's an efficient way to let people know who you are, how to contact you, your experience and credibility within your industry, and the value that you bring to the marketplace. LinkedIn profiles are also searchable through all major search engines, including Google, which greatly increases your exposure to a worldwide audience.

Just as a traditional Rolodex is a primitive contact management system [often referred to now as a CRM (customer relationship management system)], LinkedIn is a contact management system with many more bells and whistles. Your LinkedIn profile is a snapshot in time of how you would like to present yourself to the business world. You provide basic information, such as your picture, your title, the company you work for, and your contact information. And you have the ability to add much more information, including a description of your skills, your credentials, your publications, and many more options.

Think of your LinkedIn profile as a marketing tool for your brand, as well as your own personal website. It's something like an interactive résumé (that much you probably already know), but it's also much more than that. You get only one shot at making a first impression, as they say, so making sure that your profile

THE SOCIAL MEDIA SALES REVOLUTION

impresses is paramount. People make huge buying decisions based on little pieces of information, and creating a robust profile can make the difference between whether or not a potential buyer is convinced that you can help her. Huge doors of opportunity swing on little hinges.

## Turbocharging Your LinkedIn Profile

When people do searches on LinkedIn, they see a shortened version of your profile; this gives them the information they need to determine whether or not they want to expand it to see your full profile. The shortened version of your profile will show them only your picture, your name, your geographic location, your industry, and whatever you've put in your headline (usually your job title). Your full version will have all this and as much more as you'd like to add to create as robust a profile as possible. You're in sales—you already know how short your buyer's attention span is! Maximize the shortened version in order to increase the likelihood that the buyer will review your full profile. Use as much of the available space as possible to paint the most descriptive picture of yourself that you can. This is a small but important aspect of your online identity that pays dividends.

Next, create a compelling headline that gives more than just your job title. Think in terms of marketing; stand out from the crowd. In your title, create a descriptive message of how you deliver value to your clients. Maximize the available characters to make it sizzle. Instead of stating "Sales Representative," say something like "Sales Representative with 10 Years' Experience and a Proven Track Record of Overdelivering." You can modify your headline as many times as you like, so don't feel that you have to get it absolutely perfect. Your LinkedIn profile will always be a work in progress, and as such, it is just a snapshot in time of who you are. Just remember to stay focused on making it as appealing as possible.

There is space in your profile for a picture. Be sure to add a headshot of yourself smiling. Being seriously successful doesn't have to mean that you look seriously intimidating or, worse, angry. Being successful in business and being friendly are not mutually exclusive. Make sure you appear approachable. Don't post a picture of yourself sneering with Donald Trump–like arrogance. (Check that hair, too, now that we think about it.) Use an image that shows your full face. You may also want to use this shot across all your social media accounts to create a consistent image of who you are.

*Status Update*

In your Status Update section, post a link to an interesting article that you think your network will see value in. Don't promote your product or service here. People don't want to log on to LinkedIn and be assaulted with sales pitches. They want information that will help them with specific concerns. Whenever users log on to LinkedIn, they will see the most recent status updates of their 1st [Degree] Connections in chronological order, with the most recent at the top. Because of your status update, even if people don't click on your link when they log on to LinkedIn, they will see your name and the link. This increases your top of mind awareness. Remember: out of sight, out of mind. Keep your name in front of people while adding value through interesting content.

## *Your Summary*

Your Summary section is critical. Here is where you have the chance to really explain who you are and why people should be interested in doing business with you. Most salespeople leave a lot of money on the table when it comes to their LinkedIn profiles. They don't maximize their use of the space available on their profile, leaving out important information and in some cases not even having anything written in the Summary section. As a result, people's profiles often look as if they were slapped together at 3:00 a.m. after a few tequilas. This doesn't serve anyone well; it marks you as an apathetic spectator in the LinkedIn community. Don't make this mistake. Use as much of the allotted space available as possible to make the right impression.

Another important point: use keywords in your summary that make it easy for people to find you in searches. First and foremost, LinkedIn is a database. Every day, more and more executives are becoming educated on its search capabilities. This means that people who make buying decisions will be searching for someone like you. Use keywords that they are likely to be using when they're searching for someone with your background and expertise. Use both industry terms and layman's terms. By strategically using certain keywords in your profile, you increase your ranking in searches. Don't just use industry jargon. Use words that express the pain that people are experiencing when they are searching for someone who can remove that pain.

Here's a power tip for putting your Summary section together: one significant feature that LinkedIn currently lacks is a spell-check. You can be the brightest person in the room, but if someone finds a bunch of spelling errors in your profile, he's not going to be thinking Mensa. The solution? Take extra care to avoid any grammatical errors or typos in your profile. First write out everything you are going to include in your LinkedIn profile in Word, and then copy and paste that information onto the site. Problem solved. Otherwise, you might want to use a browser like Firefox, which has a built-in spell-check.

## Specialties

Use the Specialties section as a place to "tag" yourself appropriately. Tagging is just adding keywords to your profile. The tags become clickable links that pull up the profile of a person who has that particular tag in his Specialties section. You already know that customization is one of the most powerful buying factors that customers use when they make purchase decisions. Get on the other side of the table, with your customer, and think about how people will be searching for you and the types of categories that they will be looking in. Build your Specialties section around these points.

*Experience*

It's important that you list not only where you currently work but also all the relevant positions you've ever had. By relevant, we mean any place where you worked for more than a few months and where you parted ways with the company amicably. By listing all these companies, you paint a clear picture of your past, and you also increase your likelihood of reconnecting with former bosses, colleagues, and clients. If you left on good terms, then you can use the Recommendation feature on LinkedIn to secure a recommendation from a former employer or client to add to your profile. The more people who can vouch for you, the better, as we will discuss later.

In your Experience section, write complete, descriptive explanations of your current and former positions. Most people don't do this; they just list their job titles and the dates when they held the position. Again, this is the herd mentality, and salespeople who do this are missing out. Always paint a clear description of yourself. Make it easy for people to learn about you. By doing so, you become interesting. You're initiating a know-like-trust relationship without having to even be there physically. Let your LinkedIn profile work for you. List any awards or special achievements associated with your various positions. Ask yourself: what information about me would a buyer find indicative that I am an expert in my field? Don't be shy; this is your chance to shine!

List all educational institutions that you attended, including your high school. This is an opportunity to reconnect with former schoolmates. In addition, people who are interested in doing business with you will be naturally curious. They will always look over this information.

## Key Applications and How to Use Them

Add applications to your profile. LinkedIn applications enable you to enrich your profile, share and collaborate with your network, and get the key insights that help you be more effective. LinkedIn is constantly adding to the number of available applications. A few to be aware of are Box.net Files, WordPress, Company Buzz, and SlideShare Presentations.

### Box.net Files

Add the Box.net Files application to manage all your important files online. Box.net lets you share content on your profile and collaborate with friends and colleagues. You can add anything that is digital to a Box.net file. This could include sales collateral, marketing materials, white papers, customer testimonials, and other such information. By adding content to your Box.net file, you're already presenting something of value to the person who is viewing your profile. That's a good way to start a relationship.

### WordPress

Connect your virtual lives with the WordPress LinkedIn application. With the WordPress app, you can sync your WordPress blog posts with your LinkedIn profile, keeping everyone you know in the know. When someone sees the WordPress application on your profile, he is seeing a shortened version of the content that is on your blog. If this piques his interest, he can click on it, and it opens a new window that is a link to your actual blog. This is a simple method of getting people to visit your blog.

## Company Buzz

Do you ever wonder what people are saying about your company? You should; if you are a salesperson, discussions about your firm can affect your personal success. Although we'll discuss Twitter in a lot more depth in a later chapter, it's important to know that a lot of people use it as a platform for talking about various companies. It'll suffice for now to say that Twitter is an excellent way to stay on top of what people are saying, and Company Buzz shows you the Twitter activity associated with your company. View tweets, trends, and top keywords. Customize your topics and share with your coworkers.

## SlideShare Presentations

SlideShare is the best way to share presentations on LinkedIn. You can upload and display your own presentations, check out presentations from your colleagues, and find experts within your network. Very few people utilize the video capabilities of this application. Adding video to your profile creates a huge difference between you and your competitors. You can add a video of you explaining who you are and your credentials, a company marketing video, client testimonials, or whatever you like that is relevant. This allows prospective buyers to get familiar with you, who you are, and what you bring to the table in a safe, noncommittal environment before they ever take the step of meeting you. You're limited only by your imagination. Can you say "free commercial"?

*Recommendations*

Being a salesperson, you already know the power that having a client write you a testimonial letter has in favorably influencing a buying decision. As Landy discussed in his book *Competitive Selling,* having a significant set of endorsements from people who have worked with you successfully is a key to showing proof of performance, because having this documentation reduces the perceived risk for people who are considering doing business with you. Kevin certainly gets this point; at the time of this writing, he literally has the most LinkedIn endorsements of anyone in the world, and by a wide margin. That should tell you something about the importance that needs to be placed on this section of your profile.

The Recommendation section of your LinkedIn profile addresses this key issue, and it is one of the most important sections of your profile. Like everyone else's, your profile is biased toward what you perceive as your strengths. After all, you wrote it. Having the ability to showcase written testimonials from coworkers, managers, and clients is a real game changer. What you are essentially saying to those who view your recommendations is: "Don't take my word for it that I'm good at what I do; take a gander at what my customers say." Having said that, it is absolutely amazing to us that more people don't leverage this section of their LinkedIn profile. The fact is that the vast majority of users don't.

When people compare your profile with the profiles of other salespeople in your industry and you have people stating that they have done business with you and had favorable outcomes, you have shifted the odds in your favor in a major way. Also be aware that you must approve all recommendations before they are shown on your profile, so you never have to worry about being dissed via an unfavorable recommendation. You have the power to always present yourself in the most positive light in your profile.

Never be afraid to ask for a recommendation from someone who is in a position to write one for you. After all, you've earned it. Most people will be flattered that you asked. By asking the person to recommend you, you are letting her know that you value her opinion. Remember that what comes around, goes around; make sure that you are also willing to write recommendations for people whom you are in a position to recommend.

Finally, you'll want to include your contact information at the bottom of your LinkedIn profile so buyers who wish to get in touch with you can do so with ease. It doesn't serve you well as a sales professional in the twenty-first century to appear to be in the Witness Relocation Program. Make it easy for people to find you and communicate with you.

## Managing Contacts

Your LinkedIn account is essentially your online, real-time Rolodex. It is essentially the largest database of business professionals ever created. Not only is it the best business networking database in the world, but it also makes visible the hidden connections between people whom you know and people whom you don't, connections that you didn't even know you already had. How cool is that? The importance of this cannot be overemphasized. This functionality does not exist in exactly the same way on Facebook or Twitter. The ease with which LinkedIn gives you this information is amazing. To professional salespeople who understand that all long-term sales success is built on relationships, this is awfully important. For salespeople, relationships are the ultimate sales catalyst.

We've all heard of the whole "six degrees of separation" concept, perhaps in the form of the Kevin Bacon game, which says that everyone on earth is connected to everyone else by no more than six people. This concept implies that as we all become increasingly connected, the world is getting smaller. It's true. The irony is that it's often a lot less than six degrees removed from other people, regardless of geography.

LinkedIn works in three degrees of separation. It shows you the connections that your connections have. Not only do you have a database of people to whom you're connected, but you now have a database of people to whom *they're* connected. Get it? Now, we're not saying that the old days of smiling and dialing, getting past the gatekeeper, building rapport, and "Oh, my, did you catch that fish on the wall?" are completely over—at least not yet. You can do that if you wish, but if you want to blow your sales numbers out of the water, you need to recognize that when it comes to generating new business, building referrals is a heck of a lot more productive than making cold calls.

## Reaching "Critical Mass": A Key to Success

Building a large network of LinkedIn connections is critical to your maximizing the full power of LinkedIn as a sales tool. Some people ask the "quantity versus quality" question: do I want to be picky when it comes to those that I choose to connect with? This is a logical concern. In our opinion, it's not an "either/or" situation, but rather an "and" one. By building a network that combines both quality and quantity contacts, you exponentially increase the likelihood that there will be some form of connection to the people and companies that you'd like to sell to. It's largely a numbers game.

In the Add Connections section, you have multiple ways to link more people to your account. LinkedIn integrates with all major e-mail platforms, including Gmail and Outlook. By permitting it to reconcile all the e-mail addresses associated with the more than 110,000,000 existing LinkedIn users with all the e-mail addresses in your e-mail address book, you can see whom you've e-mailed in the past who already has a LinkedIn profile. This is a major time saver when it comes to building your network. These individuals will be shown in alphabetical order, and you can select the ones that you'd like to send a LinkedIn Invitation Request to. You can also send invitations to people who are not already on LinkedIn. You can also upload contacts from CSV files, ACT, and other sources.

Since LinkedIn is a massive database, and since you've created a robust profile that indicates where you went to school and where you've worked, now you can see which of the people that you went to school with and whom you've worked with are already on board. LinkedIn will show you all the people who have the same schools and places of employment in their profile.

Every connection that you have increases the value of your LinkedIn network. Never forget that at the end of the day, whom you know is more important that what you know. Many of your former classmates, for example, probably know nothing about what you do for a living. Once they do, who is to say when they may give your name to a business colleague who is in the market for what you sell?

Back in the previous century, we had little black books with all our phone numbers in them. No matter how good we were at staying in touch, though, sooner or later those friends fell off the face of the earth. Until recently, there was really no way of finding them again without hiring a detective. Those days are over. As a matter of fact, kids today probably can't even imagine a world in which you could ever lose track of someone. We've come a long way in a short time.

As mentioned earlier, most salespeople use some form of CRM solution. Salesforce.com is one of the best known and most used sales CRM solutions. It can be integrated with LinkedIn, and it makes sense that more CRM solutions will soon be integrating with LinkedIn. If you have a contact in Salesforce.com, you can automatically see his LinkedIn Profile. Talk about tremendous sales intelligence!

## The Etiquette of Making Connections

When you send someone an invitation to connect on LinkedIn, don't do what almost everyone does and simply send the standard template message. If you want to have a high success rate in connecting, you should create a customized invitation. As you will soon see, it takes only a moment, and it has a profound impact. Make sure to get across the message that you'd like to create a mutually beneficial, win-win relationship with this person and that you'd like to add value to her professional network, but be sure to phrase it in your own voice and to be friendly. No one likes corporate-sounding messages, and coming across like you are a run-of-the-mill sales drone is no way to start or rekindle a relationship.

A major time saver when customizing invitations is to create a "LinkedIn Related" folder on the desktop of your computer. In this folder, you will have a number of Word documents that are templates, each of which can be quickly and easily customized to a particular contact and situation. Depending on whom you're connecting with, you can probably change only a few words and still have the invitation sound very warm and personal. Just copy and paste them, and voilà! You will stand out by connecting in a more personal manner.

When someone sends you a LinkedIn invitation request, make sure that after you accept his invitation, you take a moment to send him a personal message. After all, if someone said hello to you at a live networking event, you'd acknowledge him, wouldn't you? So you should do the same thing online. Sending a nice message thanking the person for the invitation, explaining a little bit about what you do for a living, and asking how you can help him in some way isn't being "salesy"; it is being considerate. Why should you do this? Because most people don't bother, and doing so will make you stand out.

One last point about making connections: take your selling hat off. Many sales trainers teach A-B-C, which stands for "always be closing." That's old hat and has no place here; no one wants to be "closed." We also teach A-B-C, but for us, it stands for "always be connecting." Never pass up an opportunity to make a personal connection. In a more and more interconnected world, you never know where your next client or referral source is going to come from. Always be connecting.

# Advanced Search

As a sales professional, you know your targeted demographic in terms of industry, title of the buyer, geography, and any of a number of other variables. In olden times (pre-Internet), we used to rely on a number of information sources, such as Hoovers (a market research database that salespeople could pay for) and other databases that charged for sales information. What can be accomplished with LinkedIn makes those old ways of gathering information look like a horse and buggy.

LinkedIn has a screen called Advanced Search. This is a tool with which you can populate many fields, including keywords, first name, last name, title, company, school, location, country, postal code, industry, relationship, language, company size, seniority level, interested in, Fortune ranking, and other parameters. By strategically using the Advanced Search function, you can pinpoint people with a laserlike accuracy that would have been unheard of not too many years ago. LinkedIn searches through the 110,000,000 LinkedIn profiles and lists the people who fit your parameters. You can save searches in folders and receive daily e-mail alerts when new people match your search criteria. This is an excellent form of time management. LinkedIn becomes in some ways a CRM solution if you're not already using a CRM solution. And again, LinkedIn can already be integrated with Salesforce.com and Outlook.

## Power Play: Getting Introduced

Because LinkedIn works in three degrees of separation, and because LinkedIn reveals the hidden connections that you didn't even know you had, you can now see how you're connected to these targeted people through mutual connections. There is a button labeled "Get Introduced Through a Connection" that acts as a medium between you and the people you would like to meet. Why would you ever take the time and energy to create and try to deliver scintillating traditional voice mail and e-mail messages that are never going to be looked at or listened to, let alone returned, when you could get a warm introduction through a mutual connection?

Consider the implications for a moment: you can create a message and send it to your mutual connection, who then can forward it to the targeted prospect. You can also create a message for the mutual connection asking her to forward your message. The mutual connection can see what you've written to the targeted prospect, so she can ensure that she feels comfortable forwarding the message. The mutual connection can't modify your message, but she can add an extra note for the targeted prospect, thereby giving you a warm introduction.

This reveals what we think is an interesting paradox regarding social media. There are a lot of people who seem to think, "I'll just get connected to everybody and his brother on LinkedIn, Facebook, and Twitter, and the clouds will part and the money will just fall out of the sky." It does not exactly work like that. In fact, it does not work that way at all. That is a passive and naïve view of the way business is done. After all, if having a large database of names and numbers ensured riches, then everybody with a phone book should be a millionaire.

No matter how many connections you have, it's still going to come down to your networking skills, interpersonal skills, and sales skills. LinkedIn may show you the doors, but those skills are still going to be required if you are to open those doors and walk through them. Becoming a social media guru isn't going to turn you into a sales superstar. You're still going to need great sales chops. So for every minute that you're spending learning how to use social media as a sales tool, make sure you're spending a corresponding minute sharpening your sales ax. That aspect of your job isn't going to change, no matter how much further technology takes us.

After training hundreds of organizations and many thousands of salespeople over the past eight years on the most effective uses of LinkedIn as a sales tool, it's been very gratifying to hear people tell us that they were able to close sales of up to $500,000 by using LinkedIn—and then to add that they never would have been able to build a relationship with that client had it not been for LinkedIn.

## Companies

There was a time, not that long ago, when you could learn only about individuals on LinkedIn. Now you can also do your due diligence on companies, and other people can find information on your company. You can add your company to LinkedIn by creating a profile for it. A Company page has four tabs: "Overview," "Careers," "Products & Services," and "Analytics" (visible to company administrators only). Your company can utilize many areas of the page for free, although there are premium services, as you'll see later.

As a sales professional, you're dependent on your market research. LinkedIn Companies is a great way to get up-to-date, highly valuable market research. You can browse industries or

THE SOCIAL MEDIA SALES REVOLUTION

search for specific companies. When you identify a company that you'd like to learn more about on an updated basis, you can "follow" the company, and LinkedIn will e-mail you updated data on a regular basis. This allows you to stay completely up to date on new products, personnel changes, and other news without lifting a finger. You can also see who else is following the company. Since following other companies can help you keep tabs on your competitors, you may want to see who's following *your* company.

LinkedIn automatically lists all current and former employees associated with the company that you're interested in researching. It automatically sorts them according to current or former employee, new hire, and other statuses. LinkedIn will show you your 1st and 2nd [Degree] Connections at the company and how many of its employees are on LinkedIn. The data are broken down into several categories, including "Job Functions," "University Attended," "Annual Company Growth," "Other Companies viewed by people who have looked at this company," "Departures," "Before and After Companies (where the employees work or worked)," "Geographic Breakdown," "Most Recommendations," "Job Function," "Company Size," "Website," "Industry," and "Promotional Material," among others.

That is an incredible amount of data to have at your fingertips. The days of being an uninformed salesperson are over. There's no longer any excuse not to be on top of your sales intelligence. Now you can stay informed about what's happening across the board. LinkedIn will even e-mail you the data on a weekly basis. This is a horrible time to be lazy in the face of so much data, and a great time to take advantage of it. Your game plan? Determine which industries and companies you need to stay on top of and add them to your follow list. Track and sort the information, and by doing so, you will become a better salesperson.

## Groups

Birds of a feather flock together. If you want to soar, go where the eagles are. If you could be a fly on the wall at a cocktail party of your ideal prospects, would you be interested? Welcome to LinkedIn Groups.

Joining specific groups on LinkedIn can help you stay informed and keep in touch with people who share your interests. You can join up to 50 such groups, and we suggest that you join at least 20 to 30. Make about 80 percent of the groups you join related to your profession, and about 20 percent related to your personal nonbusiness interests. Yes, LinkedIn is about business, but there are lifestyle-related groups on LinkedIn also. You like swing dancing? Why not connect with some other people who share your interest? If you're networking correctly, you never know where the conversations may go.

Watch the discussion threads on these groups. You will be observing conversations that you may be able to add value to. When you see a discussion related to something that you can help someone with, don't embarrass yourself by straight-up selling. LinkedIn Groups is not about pitching your product or service. It's about adding value and building relationships. You can have updated comments to whichever discussion threads you like e-mailed to you to keep you in the loop as to who is commenting and what they're saying. This is all about giving help to others, not helping yourself.

We're not saying that you should give away all your secret sauce or that you should give away information for free that you normally charge money for, but rather that you should build relationships that lead to revenue. People are talking about business-related things in your groups on a continual basis, and if you stay involved, this can open huge doors of opportunity for you. So be patient. Participate, but don't push. Don't kiss on the first date. Build a know-like-trust relationship.

Another power tip for participating in groups: we all receive e-mail newsletters, e-zines, and other information that could help our clients. Once a week or so, cut and paste the link to an e-zine or article, and use this to start a discussion thread in selected LinkedIn groups. Just say something as simple as, "This is an interesting article about blank, and I'd love to get your thoughts on it. I hope you get as much out of it as I did." See if people comment on it. These are more than just conversations; they become opportunities to build relationships.

You can also send messages directly to people with whom you share a LinkedIn group. This is very important. Prior to being in a group with someone, you may have been beyond the three degrees of separation and not been able to communicate with that individual without using your Inmail. With the free version of LinkedIn, you are limited to three messages that you can send to people whom you are not a 1st Connection with. These messages are called Inmail. If you belong to a group with someone, you have the ability to send a message to that person directly, as if you were a direct connection. This a major reason to fish where the fish are, so to speak.

Finally, for you hard-core types, be aware that there is a section of LinkedIn Groups called Promotions. This is where you can blatantly offer your product or service. Feel free to post things there that are shamelessly self-promotional in nature. But we would still be careful not to post too many pitches there. Take the high road. Promote yourself with discretion. People are smart, and if you're coming across like a huckster, they will sense it.

## LinkedIn Answers

LinkedIn Answers is a function that most people are probably unfamiliar with, even though it's actually one of LinkedIn's most powerful features. Major news sources watch LinkedIn Answers to determine who is a thought leader in their industry. It's basically a search engine divided into industries.

Anyone on LinkedIn can ask or answer questions related to just about anything. If you type a word or phrase into the Answers Advanced Search, you'll see every recent use of that word or phrase. If you're answering questions, people will see that, and it will help to position you as a thought leader in your industry. Make sure that your answers are not self-promotional in nature. Help people. All things being equal, people do business with and refer business to people whom they know, like, and trust. We cannot overemphasize this.

Find the industry that you serve and look at what people are asking and answering. In some cases, this can be a gold mine.

Many people are asking questions and looking for your help. And they're often not covert about it. They need help. We repeat: this is a place where people aren't even shy about asking for your help. Welcome to LinkedIn Answers.

As with the LinkedIn Groups function, you can have the updated comments to whichever discussion threads you're following in answers sent to you on a continual basis so you can see how conversations are progressing and whether there are other opportunities for you to add value to the conversation.

People can indicate who they think has the best answer to each question, and you can become the recognized thought leader in your industry by providing great answers to the questions that are posed. With this tool, you aren't promoting yourself as the go-to person; other people are promoting you. People will be looking for someone who can help them, and by ranking highly as someone who frequently provides great value to others on LinkedIn Answers, you will automatically grab their attention as someone whom they should be speaking to.

## Events

Do you have an upcoming Webinar, trade show, or open house at your company? The Events section of LinkedIn is a great place to promote any upcoming events that you may have. You can create an Event notice that contains information describing your event, including a link to your website. If you have an upcoming seminar, Webinar, trade show, or any other online or offline gathering, you can let the LinkedIn community know about it. And it costs you nothing. Not one dollar.

Your prospects are looking at LinkedIn Events to determine where they can network and gather information that will help them with their businesses. When you create your event, you must indicate who you think may be interested. You can indicate CEO, CFO, HR manager, or any other title, and these people can then search LinkedIn Events by job title or keyword related to their job to see which events are coming up that they might have an interest in.

Events are divided into "Conferences," "Tradeshows & Conventions," "Networking & Meetups," "Training & Seminars," "Fundraisers," and "Other Events." Position your event in the correct section and you'll gain much more visibility.

For a nominal fee, LinkedIn also provides Premium Events. This is a new functionality that LinkedIn has introduced that allows you to post an announcement for your event in front of your ideal prospect whenever she logs in to LinkedIn. When you know who your ideal prospect is and you create a premium event, LinkedIn will showcase that event to your ideal audience with precision. Talk about targeted marketing!

This is just an overview of LinkedIn and the functionalities that are currently available. In a later chapter, we'll describe a daily routine showing how to use LinkedIn most effectively to grow your business.

## Summary

We're guessing that 10 years ago, even if you worked for the CIA, this type of information from anywhere in the world was not available at your fingertips 24/7/365. As sales professionals, we depend on information—relevant, timely information—to help us sell. LinkedIn provides you with more than enough information to separate you from the sales hacks who are still toiling in obscurity, using twentieth-century sales methods like smiling and dialing and spamming their database with e-mails that will never be read. If you want to stand out, it's time to get on board.

Spending a little bit of time to create a robust profile and learning how to use LinkedIn most effectively will provide you with great sales opportunities.

Just as working out once a month isn't going to make much of a difference to your body and will probably just make you sore, visiting LinkedIn once a month isn't going to do much for you. We suggest that you visit LinkedIn every day, just like you check your e-mail every day. We will talk about this in more depth in a later chapter. For now, wrap your brain around the idea of using LinkedIn every day. A few minutes a day on LinkedIn, with time and commitment, will produce amazing results. If you're not using LinkedIn on a daily basis, how will you know about the opportunities that are there for you?

We can teach you all the great ways in which LinkedIn can help your career and your bank account, but at the end of the day, it's still up to you. You would think that all salespeople would be jumping on board like a pit bull on a mailman. Nope. You would also think that since we know that drinking and smoking aren't good for us, no one would drink or smoke. Nope again. Knowing and not doing is actually the same as not knowing.

After years and years of achieving top results in our sales careers and training salespeople all over the world, we've learned one thing for sure: giving a lazy or unmotivated salesperson the best training and tools does not turn that salesperson into a top performer. There are no magic bullets. If there were, every sales manager in the world would have his pistol full of them.

The good news is that for salespeople who are professionals and who are sincerely interested in making themselves and their company excel, there has never been a better time to be in sales. The tools we have at our disposal now are beyond anything that we could have imagined a few years ago. And here's the kicker: it takes so little to be above average—both within your organization and to your prospects.

By using LinkedIn effectively, you are conveying to your prospects that you are a professional who is worthy of their time and their business. Perception is reality. How your prospects and your referral partners view you is critical. You now have available to you everything you need to position yourself as the professional that you are. So don't just set up your account and walk away; you are wasting your time by doing so. If you want to get your sales numbers in tip-top shape, schedule time to "work out" on a daily basis.

Small activities repeated over time produce amazing results—any top sales performer will tell you so. There's a paradox, though. Most people think they have to make massive, dramatic changes in the ways that they do things in order to create results. That is a myth. Just use LinkedIn to its potential on a daily basis, and over time you will grow sales muscles that you wouldn't believe. If you're not LinkedIn, you're linked out.

CHAPTER 3

# HOW TO GET RESULTS WITH TWITTER

## Tapping into Global Conversations

There are many people who wonder what kind of value Twitter has for anyone, and a lot of them are sales professionals. At first glance, this is understandable. When we are conducting a seminar, we often ask the audience, "Who thinks that Twitter is just 13-year-olds talking about what they had for lunch?" Without fail, a large portion of the audience put their hands up. Then we say, "If you think that Twitter has 13-year-olds talking about what they had for lunch . . . you are absolutely correct." And we let that sink in, before continuing, "But let's agree that the telephone is also about 13-year-olds talking about what they had for lunch." The point, of course, is that the telephone has many other uses, too.

Twitter is a communication tool like the telephone, but about two hundred million times more powerful. Why? Because unlike a phone, which allows you to talk with one person at a time, Twitter lets you communicate simultaneously with anyone from one to more than two hundred million people. As with the other applications discussed in this book, we recommend that, to get maximum value from this chapter, you go to www.twitter.com, create an account if you have not already done so, log in, and follow along with us.

## Who's on Twitter?

According to the company itself, the fastest-growing demographic on Twitter is 35- to 45-year-olds. Twitter is not just for kids. There are millions of business professionals on Twitter, and millions more are joining each week.

Twitter is the best real-time communication tool the world has ever seen. If you doubt that statement, here's the proof. Remember when the terrorists stormed that luxury hotel in India a few years ago? People using Twitter were the first ones to alert the police. Remember the Miracle on the Hudson plane landing? People using Twitter were the first ones to let the rest of the world know what was happening. No matter where it happens in the world, news is likely to show up on Twitter before it appears on CNN!

The old days of society being dependent on traditional media companies for news are over, and the media companies are very aware of it. They can no longer control the flow of information and provide only what they choose. Actually, they can, but the problem they face is that people are tuning them out and getting their news from other sources, such as Twitter. Having other options effectively turns every human being with a cell phone into a one-person media company.

People who have large followings—musicians, athletes, and other media figures—can take advantage of their enormous reach through Twitter. As of this writing, people such as Oprah Winfrey and Ashton Kutcher can, and do, broadcast whatever they want, whenever they want, to millions and millions of people in an instant from their cell phone. In some ways, the Internet is kind of like a giant electronic bulletin board. As on any bulletin board, you're going to find the good, the bad, and the ugly on the Internet; Twitter is no different. You don't want to throw the baby out with the bathwater, though. It's important, then, to be strategic about which information we choose to receive and which information we choose to send out.

In our speaking engagements, we often refer to LinkedIn, Facebook, and Twitter as the Big Three. No one is going to argue with the idea that these three social networking platforms have edged out many other social networking sites as the key resources online. Of the Big Three, Twitter is by far the easiest to learn, the easiest to use, and the fastest to get up and actively participating.

# How, and Why, Twitter Works

In essence, Twitter is just global text messaging, with links thrown in. You use it by broadcasting a text message of 140 characters or less, called a *tweet*, to other Twitter users. You can also "follow" people, which means that you are able to read their tweets, while other people correspondingly follow you and are able to read your tweets. That's Twitter in its simplest form. It gets much more interesting and valuable than that as you go deeper and deeper down the rabbit hole. And like Alice, you can see some pretty amazing things down that rabbit hole.

Everyone knows that he can search for whatever he is looking for on Google and find some information about it. Well, what if you could see what two hundred million people are saying about whatever it is that you're interested in? What if you could monitor conversations based on keywords like your name, your company's name, or your competitor's name or product; keywords related to pains that your product or service solves; or any number of other things that you'd like to keep your finger on the pulse of? Welcome to the business power of Twitter.

As we have said repeatedly throughout this book, we are in no way advocating or promoting stalking or invading people's privacy. It is important that we mention that again here. Social networking is by definition "social," and the things that people are talking about on most social networking platforms are visible to the other people on those platforms. After all, if the public is having a conversation about your company anyway, don't you want to be a part of the conversation? As with LinkedIn and Facebook, we could write an entire book on Twitter. For the purpose of this chapter and the relevance of Twitter to salespeople, though, we will just cover the basics of how Twitter works and focus on your profile, whom to follow and gaining followers, what to tweet about, and monitoring tweets.

## Your Profile

On Twitter, you have a user name, or *handle*, to identify yourself. We usually recommend that you use your real name, although there is a fair chance that someone will have already taken it, in which case you'll have to customize a bit, using abbreviations or a number. Twitter doesn't allow you to put a space between your first and last names, but you can put an underscore between them if you like. You can capitalize your first and last names, but people will still be able to find you whether they capitalize when searching or not. Also, make sure that your Twitter name is as short as possible. You'll understand why when we talk about how every character that you type into Twitter is important.

Make sure that you create a user name that is separate from your company's name. You may find this shocking, but you might not be working at your current job for the rest of your life. Using your name or some variation of your name allows you to let your Twitter account follow you regardless of who's cutting your commission checks. You can also add a link to a website on your profile to give potential followers a chance to find out more information about you. You may want to use your LinkedIn Public Profile URL as your website so when someone is checking you out on Twitter, she can also connect with you on LinkedIn. The salespeople who use social media most effectively connect with people on as many social networking platforms as they can.

Unlike LinkedIn and Facebook, where you can create a very robust profile, Twitter allows you only a brief profile bio of 160 characters to explain who you are. Twitter is definitely not *War and Peace*. No one has time for that. With an economy of characters, paint a descriptive picture of who you are and what you do for a living. You have only a few seconds to grab people's attention here, so by all means make it compelling. If you want to change it at any time, you can. As with so many other things related to social networking, nothing is written in stone here. Treat your Twitter profile bio as a constant work in progress.

Upload a smiling headshot of yourself, not a corporate logo. Logos are for companies, not people. There are uses for corporate Twitter accounts, but we are talking about your personal Twitter account here. You are representing yourself in this environment, not your company. Don't forget to smile. As obvious as it may sound, many people forget that everyone makes very quick value judgments about other people all the time. Knowing that Twitter is all about brevity, access to speed of information, make sure that you are extending your hand in friendship by smiling. The point is simple but obvious: always be friendly and approachable.

To stand out from the crowd, we suggest that you create a Twitter background for your account. A background is the blank space on the sides of your Twitter account. This is online real estate that you can be using to help people learn more about you. Go to Google and do a search on "free twitter backgrounds," and you will find plenty of free services to create your Twitter background and make it memorable.

You should also add your contact information to your background, so that when someone is looking at your profile, he can see multiple ways in which to communicate and connect with you. Unlike other applications, your contact information here will appear as a clickable link, and that makes it easy for people to reach you. You can also add pictures of yourself or anything else you would like (within the limits of good taste, of course). Represent yourself in the most professional manner possible, and always err on the conservative side.

You should also activate Twitter on your cell phone so you can access Twitter while you're out and about. Being able to communicate on Twitter from anywhere is a huge part of its value. Capitalizing on this requires the capability to be available on your mobile device. After all, that is really what Twitter is all about: the ability to communicate and listen to communications from wherever you are. If the only time you can access Twitter is when you are in front of your computer, this really defeats the purpose of having a Twitter account in the first place. Another self-defeating action is creating a profile that is locked to people you don't know. Make sure that you don't accidentally "lock" your Twitter account and make it private. The goal here is to be accessible and not too difficult to find.

You may or may not want to add the location function to your Twitter account. We personally don't do that with our Twitter accounts, because nobody needs to know the exact location from which we are sending our tweets. This is one aspect of social media that has shades of Big Brother. If you want the world to know every single thing about you, using social media certainly allows you to do so. Geolocation services like Foursquare have opened up great business opportunities for companies that leverage them strategically, but you may not want everyone to know that you're sending tweets from Atlanta when you live in Los Angeles. Can you say "Hello, Mr. Burglar"?

Once you have opened your Twitter account, you should go to www.twellow.com and activate an account listing. Twellow is short for "Twitter Yellow Pages." This gives you the opportunity to create a much more robust profile, similar to those available on LinkedIn and Facebook, where people who read your information can get a much better understanding of who you are and what value you bring to the marketplace. Here, you select the industries and interests that you would like your profile to be associated with, which opens up a whole world of people who have interests similar to yours.

## Whom to Follow and Gaining Followers

Once you've set up your Twitter account, you need, of course, to start following people. Twitter has magical algorithms at work that offer suggestions as to whom you may want to follow based on your profile's keywords and location. You can click on these people's names and see their profiles, view what they tweet about, and decide whether or not they are people whom you would like to follow.

"Following" someone does not mean that you're stalking her. It just means that when she posts a tweet (one of those messages of 140 characters or fewer), it will show up in your Twitter news feed. Your news feed is nothing more than a chronological listing of the tweets of the people you're following, with the most recent at the top.

When you are following someone, you are being kept up to date on whatever that person is tweeting. If you follow a diverse group of people, your experience with Twitter will be interesting and varied. Don't worry too much about whether people follow you back when you follow them; rest assured, you will eventually grow your own group of followers.

Twitter allows you to enter your e-mail address and, in a manner similar to the way in which Facebook and LinkedIn operate, will reconcile the e-mail addresses in your Gmail, AOL, Hotmail, and Yahoo! e-mail accounts to find which of your contacts are also among Twitter's two hundred million existing users.

This is a big time saver, and you'll be surprised at how many of your contacts already have Twitter accounts set up. You can also enter the e-mail addresses of people who are not on Twitter, and Twitter will send them an e-mail indicating that you'd like them to connect with you on Twitter. Many social networking sites are integrating with one another to help you add connections faster and more easily. The algorithms are very powerful, and when you start to follow someone, Twitter will tell you who he is similar to. In many cases, you may decide to follow these other individuals also.

The Search function is one of the most useful functions available on Twitter. Using this feature, you can search on any word, including names. This is one simple way to determine whether someone you want to follow is on Twitter. Type the person's name into the search box, with no space between the first and last names. In a lot of cases, this will provide their Twitter name. Otherwise, just try Googling the person's name and the word *Twitter*, and you might find her handle that way. On a related note, you should also search for words related to the various uses of your product or service. If people are talking about the things that your company can help with, it just makes sense to find those people and connect with them.

As much as we love Twitter, it can be like a Mercedes S600 with square tires at first; it's an amazing vehicle, and until you know that round tires exist, you don't mind the bumpy ride. Twitter is built on a type of computer code that's called open source. All that means is that anyone who has tape on his glasses and a pocket protector and who can write code has the potential to write separate programs that interact with Twitter. The fact that people can customize Twitter has opened up all kinds of innovative ways for people to use it.

We are going to show you some of the round tires that exist so that you can enjoy a smoother ride. As a matter of fact, once we show you some of these tires, you may end up not spending as much time on the actual Twitter site and spending more time on a few of these other sites that effectively drive on the Twitter chassis. Okay—enough with the car analogies.

## Using Twellow

As we briefly mentioned earlier, Twellow (www.twellow.com) is hugely helpful in determining who is valuable to follow on Twitter. Like the Yellow Pages, Twellow is a directory organized by industries, interests, and many other factors. If you're looking to connect with people in a certain vertical market, or with others who have a particular interest, it is more than likely that they are represented on Twellow. Click on a keyword and you'll be shown a listing of all the people who have identified themselves as wanting to be associated with that particular industry or having that particular interest.

The people participating on Twellow will be listed based on the number of followers they have, ranked from highest to lowest. You can then click on these individuals and see their expanded profiles and all their tweets. This is a great way to make good decisions about whom you want to follow. Prior to social networking, we could only dream about being able to find prospects who have identified themselves with this type of precision. Finding credible leads has never been easier!

Twellow also allows you to search by geographic region. This can be very helpful if you have a defined sales territory. If you click on "Twellowhood," a map of the world will load, letting you drill into any geographic area you like. It will then show you down to the city level who lives in each area and her Twitter accounts. By determining who is in the area in which you do business and then refining your search parameters based on keywords like your industry and your interests, you have just created a highly refined list of target prospects. And to reemphasize a previous point, not only can you identify these people, but you can see the links to their websites, whom they're following, who's following them, and everything they're tweeting about. When you really wrap your mind around this, you may need to take a nap. This is powerful stuff. You are now an invisible fly on the wall at the world's largest cocktail party.

## Sizing Up People to Follow

The visibility that Twitter provides concerning people, their interests, and the things they like to talk about is truly staggering. When you open someone's profile, you will see how he represents himself in terms of his bio. You will also see whether he has a Twitter background, which, in addition to giving you his contact information, gives you an indication of his familiarity with Twitter.

As you review the information, you can see how many tweets this person has sent out, and if you felt like investing the time, you could read every single tweet that he has ever sent. In addition, you can see how many people he's following and how many people are following him. Best of all, you can also see who each of these people (those who are following him and those whom he is following) is. This could be very valuable information to determine who this person considers important enough to listen to and who considers him important enough. You can "favorite" tweets so that you can go back and see them at any time, and that means that you can also see what tweets other people have "favorited." Wouldn't you get a lot of information about people by seeing what tweets they've indicated are their favorites?

Start following people and observing what they're tweeting about. It's kind of like attending a cocktail party full of people you don't know. You wouldn't go running into the middle of the room trying to draw attention to yourself, so don't do that here either. Just sit back and observe until you learn the proper "netiquette."

It is very common for people whom you are following to follow you back. Do something that your parents taught you and that so many people don't do—thank them. Be polite. It takes only a second to send them a message saying thanks for the follow, and yet few people do it. Just as in the real world, lots of relationships are started with simple courtesy.

It's also beneficial to see whom the person you are following is also following. Since it turns out that she sees value in following these people, maybe you will too. Perhaps you'll find some people whom you never would have found otherwise. This is one of the powers of social media: it reveals people, connections, and opportunities that never would have been discovered prior to social media.

# What to Tweet About

You can tweet about whatever you want to tweet about, but as with all forms of communication, a little forethought can pay off big time. Do people tweet about what they just had for lunch and which Hollywood marriage they think will end next? Yes, they do. The Internet is like an electronic bathroom wall sometimes, and people will write whatever they want on it. However, one of the reasons that top salespeople make the big bucks is that they make the best use of their time. They aren't interested in non-revenue-generating trivia during business hours. They plan, execute, and profit.

You should aim to tweet about things that your prospects, clients, networking partners, and referral sources will find value in. Tweeting about mundane things that are of interest only to you probably isn't going to gain you a lot of followers, and especially not the type of followers that you want. As we have said elsewhere in the book and we will repeat here: never forget that everything you say online affects your personal brand. You are a value generator. Always tweet value.

Of course, how you are on Twitter is probably just an extension of how you are offline. If you talk a lot about yourself offline, you'll probably talk a lot about yourself online also. If you seek to serve and provide value to people offline, you will probably seek to serve and provide value online as well. This may sound obvious, but we can assure you that it's not. People spend huge amounts of time and energy trying to master the nuances of social networking without realizing that they should be learning interpersonal and face-to-face networking nuances. Having a bajillion followers on Twitter isn't going to serve you well if the people following you aren't even taking the time to read your tweets because nine out of ten of them are about you and not about things that are of interest to your followers.

About 80 percent of your tweets should pertain to something that is of interest to your followers; then you've earned the right to have 20 percent of your tweets be blatant self-promotions. There is an endless supply of things that you can tweet that can add value. Don't think that you have to come up with all your content here, either. Remember that you can tweet links to any website. Subscribe to free newsletters and e-zines that have interesting information for your prospects. Send out tweets that say something like, "Here's an interesting article related to blank. I hope you find it worth the read," and then attach the link to the article. You can also send out a positive quote of the day to give your feed some regularity. Create Google Alerts based on keywords related to things that are of interest to your prospects—these will send you links every day related to whatever alert you've set up. You will never run out of content.

We all know how to forward an e-mail to someone. You can do something similar on Twitter, and it's one of the highest compliments that you can pay someone on Twitter. It's called the *retweet*. When you read a tweet that you think is interesting, you can retweet it to your followers. If you're tweeting out information that people find interesting, they'll probably be retweeting it to their followers. This is a great way to expand your influence and gain more followers, and ironically, it all comes back to the main idea of business networking online: adding value.

There is no one best way to use Twitter, and anyone who tells you that there is is lying. Be careful of the folks who call themselves gurus. By sending out tweets that people find interesting, you *will* gain followers, though. And if someone following you has a large number of followers and retweets your tweets, you will become visible to a much larger number of people whom you probably would never have been visible to before. This is a good reason to get followed by influential people.

Another point to remember: treat your followers with respect. If they send you a direct message, make sure that you reply with a direct message in a timely manner, just as you would by e-mail or phone. Once again, err on the conservative side. On Twitter, there is no inflection, tone of voice, or body language for people to observe when they're reading your tweets. Make sure that you're not coming across like a wise guy or as sarcastic.

Use Twitter as a tool to ask questions of your followers. It's a great way to test ideas before you go to the time and effort of implementing them. What a powerful way to leverage the knowledge of your followers! The collaborative nature of Twitter creates a strong sense of community, and you can use it to build strong offline relationships with people with whom your relationship started online.

When it comes to the issue of how frequently to tweet, there are a lot of different opinions. We suggest moderation in everything. If you're sending out tweets 20 times a day, you may be telling the Twitterverse that you have too much free time on your hands, that is, that you are not busy doing productive work. You may also be inundating your followers to the point that they may just ignore your tweets or unfollow you. Either way, it doesn't serve you well.

Having said that, we suggest that you tweet daily, if only once or twice a day. Your primary job is your sales gig, not trying to become a social networking superstar. Think about how best to use the tool without the tool using you or, worse, taking over your life. Send out a tweet in the morning around eight thirty. Most Twitter folks are checking their Twitter accounts in the morning as they are starting their day. You might send out another tweet after lunch and another right before the end of the workday. In a moment we will explain how you can send out these tweets without your even having to be at your computer or smart phone.

Realize that on Twitter, the lines between your personal life and your professional life are fuzzy. One of the more interesting aspects of social media is that they are forcing transparency. No matter where you go, there you are, and you cannot outrun your character. There is nothing wrong with sending out a tweet about your favorite sports team. As a matter of fact, having a mix of professional and personal tweets is normal. Just stay away from the controversial stuff if you're looking to gain followers and be seen as the professional that you are. There's probably no business advantage to tweeting strong political or lifestyle-related information.

## Monitoring Tweets

When you log on to Twitter, you will see the tweets of the people that you are following, with the most recent tweets at the top of your page. Twitter also gives you the ability to create lists so you can sort the people you're following into groups. This enables you to see updates from people very quickly, in an easily digestible manner. If you don't create lists, Twitter can be similar to drinking from a fire hydrant, depending on whom and how many people you are following.

When you are deciding whom to follow, you can see how frequently each person tweets. There are some people on Twitter about whom you will wonder whether they ever sleep. We've seen some accounts with more than 70,000 tweets logged. If you do the math and divide the number of their tweets by the number of days that Twitter has been in existence, you will arrive at the conclusion that some of these people definitely need to get a life. Seriously, nobody has that much interesting stuff to say to the rest of us. So realize that when you follow someone, it makes sense to put her into a list that you create so that you can digest your followers' tweets without gagging.

As we mentioned earlier, one of the great things about Twitter is that it's open source, which means that anyone can write code that can integrate with Twitter. Everyday people are creating new programs that leverage the tremendous amount of data that Twitter provides. Some of these programs are called *clients*. These are tools that increase the efficiency of using Twitter. There are many clients, but for now we'll just focus on one called Hootsuite. Using Hootsuite will greatly increase your ability to use Twitter for sales results. Hootsuite is a social media "dashboard" that enables you to read tweets, send tweets, and aggregate information in whatever configuration you like.

THE SOCIAL MEDIA SALES REVOLUTION

## Using Hootsuite

The way technology moves, something better than Hootsuite will probably come along very soon, but for now it is the best client for a sales professional's needs. Creating a free account is simple; just go to www.hootsuite.com and create it. Hootsuite will then ask you which social networking platforms you would like to integrate with your Hootsuite account. We recommend that you add your LinkedIn, Facebook, and Twitter accounts to Hootsuite. Doing this enables you to post things on your various social networking sites through Hootsuite.

It's a normal concern to think, "I'm already working 60 hours a week, and now you want me to start using all these social networking platforms? How am I ever going to find time to do this?" Fortunately, using Hootsuite will greatly reduce the amount of time that you would otherwise spend switching from site to site to try to stay on top of things.

You can create tabs in Hootsuite, and within each tab, you can create columns. First, create a tab with your name as the title. The first column is your Twitter feed, also called Home Feed. This is the same information that is in your Twitter account. Twitter is great, but it does not allow you to see multiple streams of information.

The next column in your personal tab should be Mentions. Any time anyone mentions your Twitter name, which is always preceded by the @ symbol, it will show up in this column. Whether what someone is saying about you is good, bad, or indifferent, wouldn't you want to know about it? Now you can know in real time anything that anyone on Twitter is saying about you, or about your company, if you are in charge of your company's Twitter account. This is a great way to do everything from damage control to relationship building.

We suggest that you follow the people who are mentioning you. They obviously have some interest in you, and it is just good etiquette to follow them. If they are not following you already, they probably will be when you start following them.

You will see when someone is retweeting your tweets because it will show up in your Mentions column. When you see this, take a few seconds and thank the person. It's just the polite thing to do. Look to see who the person is. Maybe it's someone you are not following, but whom you *should* be following. See if they this person has posted any interesting tweets recently and retweet them. Pay it forward.

The next column you create should be the keyword of your name. Make the keyword your name spelled exactly the way you normally spell it. Your Mentions column lists all uses of your Twitter name starting with the @ symbol, and your Keyword column gives mentions of your name without the @ symbol and with a space between your first and last names.

This column will be of high importance to you once you start using it. It shows you anything that is on Twitter that uses your name. It is like being an invisible fly on the wall at the world's largest cocktail party. As always, when someone is saying something nice about you, thank him. Look at his tweets and see if he is someone that you'd like to follow and if he has any tweets that you should retweet.

The next column will be your direct messages. These are the private messages that people send you on Twitter. You want to keep track so that you can respond in a timely manner.

You can create other tabs related to almost anything. Set up a tab based on the name of the company that you work for. In this tab, you should create columns for the name of your company, various product names, the name of your CEO, and other key-words related to your business that you'd like to keep tabs on (no pun intended).

You should create tabs with similar information regarding your competitors. Prior to social networking, we couldn't even imagine having the ability to track conversations that other people are having regarding our business, our competitors, and any other number of things that we see value in tracking.

Of course, it also makes a lot of sense to create tabs for key-words related to issues that your product or service solves. You should also create tabs related to geographic territory. As you already know, one of the attributes of the best salespeople in any industry is being considered the go-to person in their geographic area. When people expect you to know what is going on, you are in a valuable position indeed. Can you see how setting up your Hootsuite account correctly can position you as a thought leader?

From Hootsuite, you can send messages to LinkedIn and Face-book. These will show up as status updates on LinkedIn and wall posts on Facebook. Just remember that if you are going to send a message to Twitter in addition to LinkedIn and Facebook, the message should be 140 characters or fewer, or it will be cut off. This is important; you don't want to post tweets that nobody can make sense of. Of course, if you are not including Twitter in the places where you are posting the message, you write more than 140 characters.

As you see the tweets in your Hootsuite account, you can also retweet them, send direct messages to whoever is posting them (as long as the person doing so is following you), reply to a tweet and essentially create a conversation stream that people can watch, list a tweet as a favorite of yours, or even have the tweet sent to your e-mail. Additionally, you can see how many times the tweet has been retweeted.

## Other Features of Hootsuite

Let's take a minute and talk about some of the things that you can do from Hootsuite in terms of tweeting. We've already told you that you can send tweets from Hootsuite, just as you can from Twitter, but there's a lot more that you can do here. One significant feature is that you can schedule your tweets on Hootsuite. After you create your tweet, you have the option of either sending it right then or scheduling it to go out at some point in the future, down to the date and time. You can add links to websites in your tweets and have Hootsuite shorten the links so that the link doesn't take up too much of your available 140 characters. (Other than Hootsuite, bit.ly is the most popular URL-shortening website online.) You can also attach images and files or save your tweet as a draft and work on it later. This is tweeting on steroids!

So you can see how spending a few minutes in the morning figuring out what you'd like to tweet out during the day (while you're busy doing what you should be doing as a sales professional) and scheduling your tweets in Hootsuite is a great time saver. As a professional, you work by a schedule. You don't wing things; we all know that working in that way is for amateurs. Schedule a little time in the morning to load your Hootsuite account and let Hootsuite send out your tweets while you're out closing deals.

You can tweet on the fly from your smart phone throughout the day if you like, and you know that Hootsuite has your back and is working for you. Now, that's working intelligently.

For those who want to go above and beyond, you may want to familiarize yourself with the analytics side of Hootsuite. Now we're getting deep into the rabbit hole. Hootsuite allows you to see various types of information, including how many times your tweets have been retweeted, who has mentioned you, where in the world geographically your tweets are being retweeted from, and many other categories. Marketing people go crazy with this information, so if the marketing folks at your company don't already know how to use these tools, you may want to have them take you to lunch so you can teach them. Pick an expensive restaurant, and make sure they know that they are buying.

At the least, you should be monitoring which of your messages are being retweeted, because that will give you an indication as to which of those messages your followers may be seeing the most value in. Also, take the time to build relationships with the people who are retweeting your tweets. These are your ambassadors. They're promoting your material. Get to know these folks and figure out ways to help them. All things being equal, people do business with and refer business to people they know, like, and trust. As people are reading your tweets and retweeting them, you're developing a know-like-trust relationship with your followers. And that is one of the primary reasons why you're on Twitter.

# Summary

Twitter is worthy of your time. Should you spend all of your waking hours trying to monitor every piece of information that's flowing across Twitter? Of course not. But by strategically observing what the people whom you find important are talking about, you will uncover many selling opportunities. So, at the end of the day, it really comes down to listening, and isn't that ironic? That's exactly what professional selling has always been about and always will be about.

You can now listen to conversations on just about anything with minute precision. If you want to know which CEO in Boise has mentioned lasagna in the last month, you can see it. But do so only if that would be useful to you. Excuse us for using strange examples to prove our points.

Figure out what is worthy of tracking. Figure out what the people you would like to do business with find interesting and valuable. Figure out whom you should be paying attention to. Figure out how to deliver information that will cause people to want to follow you. Figure out how to start relationships online, then make the transition to offline relationships.

Spend some time learning the basics and advanced uses of Twitter, and position yourself as the thought leader and go-to person in your industry. Having other people toot your horn is much more effective than tooting your own horn. Use Twitter correctly and people will be seeking you out for the opportunity to do business with you.

# CHAPTER 4

# THE ROLE OF FACEBOOK IN BUSINESS DEVELOPMENT

## This Time, It's Personal

In this chapter, we'll be discussing the 800-pound gorilla of social networking sites. Facebook has become to social media what the Beatles are to rock and roll: it is the standard bearer. As of this writing, if Facebook were a country, it would be the third largest country in the world—right behind China and India, and right before the United States. That's *big*.

## If You're Going to Fish, Go Where the Fish Are

The average Facebook user spends 55 minutes per day on the site. Yes, you read that right—55 minutes per day. That's not time spent on the Internet, mind you; that's just time spent on Facebook. When you consider that much of this "face time" was previously spent in front of the television, you begin to realize why advertising dollars are flocking to the Internet. Companies spend billions of dollars each year trying to get 55 *seconds* of your attention. So if you're going to go fishing for business, you may as well go where the fish are. Right now, they are on Facebook.

You might find it interesting to learn that the fastest-growing demographic on Facebook is that of women over 55. This does not mean that only women over 55 are on Facebook, of course; everyone is there, and, as with other social media sites, the numbers are growing by the minute across all demographics. Need proof that Facebook has taken over the world of social media? Here are some stats from Facebook:

- Approximately 1 out of 13 people on earth is an active Facebook user, and half of them are logged in on any given day.
- A full 48 percent of 18- to 34-year-old adults log on to Facebook as soon as they wake up in the morning.
- About 28 percent of users check Facebook on their smart phones before getting out of bed.
- The 35-plus demographic now represents more than 30 percent of the entire Facebook user base.
- There are 207 million Internet users in the United States, which means that more than 71 percent of the U.S. Web audience is on Facebook. You read that right: 71 percent of the U.S. Web audience.
- About 57 percent of people now spend more time talking to people online than they do in person.
- A full 48 percent of young Americans say that they get their news through Facebook.
- A record-breaking 750 million photos were uploaded to Facebook over New Year's weekend 2011.
- For every 20 minutes of Facebook activity, there are 1 million links shared, 1,323,000 photos tagged, 1,484,000 event

invitations, 1,851,000 status updates, 1,972,000 friend requests accepted, 1,587,000 wall posts, 2,716,000 photos uploaded, 10,208,000 comments made, and 2,716,000 messages sent.

Have you also noticed a shift in the advertising on television lately? Many companies now end their television commercials with their Facebook fan page instead of their website. It doesn't take a rocket scientist to figure out why this is the case. It's because they know that their potential customers are on Facebook, and they want to expand their presence there as much as possible.

The massive growth that Facebook has achieved over the past few years has been nothing short of breathtaking, and the pace is quickening. When you realize that more and more people around the world are going online every day, there seems to be no end to how much it might expand. If for no other reason, Facebook needs to be a part of your business social networking strategy because of its pervasiveness in our society.

## Different Playing Field

Let's be very clear about something: Facebook is not LinkedIn or Twitter. It is a different animal. The difference is this: about 99 percent of the people on Facebook are not there to buy something. They are there to keep in touch with their friends and family by sharing information and pictures with one another. This is the most social of the social networking sites, so you have to be very careful about how you use it. Just as in real life, when people are getting together to socialize, they aren't very keen on being sold something.

It's important for you, as a business-to-business marketer, to recognize that the way people interact on Facebook is different from the way they interact on LinkedIn and Twitter. Most people are on Facebook to have social fun. They hang out, make friends, flirt, observe one another, and do a million other things that people do when they are enjoying one another's company. In a way, Facebook is kind of like the world's largest high school reunion: although everyone is there under the same banner, each participant has his own reasons for showing up. Some are there to meet friends, some are there to catch up, some are there out of sheer curiosity, and so on. We all have our individual motivations.

Just a few years ago, when you finished high school or college or stopped working for a company, you might have lost track of the people that you came into contact with during that phase of your life and gone on to the next phase, where you met new people. This fact of life was simply a given; that's the way the world was. Facebook has changed that. Now we have the ability to connect, reconnect, and stay connected. It might make things more complicated, but it can also make them more fun. Nobody ever really disappears these days.

## Facebook Basics

As with LinkedIn and Twitter, when you open your Facebook account, using the tools it gives you to find people that you know is fairly simple. A very useful business-contact feature is that you can reconcile your e-mail accounts to see which of your contacts are there already. Like all the other social networking sites, Facebook has algorithms running that see the hidden links among the people you know, and, like LinkedIn, it recommends people to you that you may want to connect with. The terms used to describe whom you know may vary among the social networking sites, but the basic concept (and benefit) is the same: on LinkedIn you have connections, on Twitter you have followers, and on Facebook you have friends.

One suggestion that we make with regard to Facebook is to have two separate accounts: one for your personal life and one for your business networking needs. You might consider calling your business account "Your Name/Company" or "Your Name/Business" to make this distinction. There are a couple of good reasons for this separation, and they revolve around the issue of mixing business with pleasure—or, more accurately, *not* doing that! The first reason is that the socializing you do with your nonbusiness friends and family is obviously of a different nature from your social life in the business world. Unless you want your clients to view old photos of you and read messages posted by your old flames, your college drinking buddies, and your Aunt Martha, it's best not to mix business with your personal life. Furthermore, from a more practical standpoint, when it comes to being a value generator, there is going to be a lot of information in your personal account that has no relevance to people whom you wish to do business with.

As you're "friending" businesspeople on Facebook, you should take a look at who your other contacts are (the ones that you might not do business with directly) and get connected to them. Part of the appeal of social networking is the surprise factor—you never know who might end up helping you out in business. As you start adding friends, Facebook, like LinkedIn, will suggest other people that you may be interested in connecting with. It might seem a little creepy at first, like a human lottery, but that's just powerful algorithms at work.

Facebook is also frequently changing its privacy settings and page design options, among many other things. This can be a little frustrating, and, as of this writing, these changes at Facebook are often in the news. Be sure to familiarize yourself with the current privacy settings. Set them to whatever level you feel comfortable with. Some people treat their lives on Facebook as an open book, and some are much more private about themselves. We all have a comfort level regarding disclosure. When it comes to your business account, just realize that being too private usually means that you will miss opportunities from people who want their business a little more straightforward.

In this chapter, we will cover some of the ways in which you should consider using Facebook for sales purposes, but there are huge differences between how business-to-business (B2B) and business-to-consumer (B2C) salespeople should view Facebook. It's a slippery slope. Let's get started by exploring your profile, groups, fan pages, and Facebook ads.

## Your Profile

As a professional salesperson, the first thing you should ask yourself is, "What is my goal in using Facebook?" For our purposes, let's agree that we want to use it to accumulate new prospects and customers and engage with existing ones. Just as with LinkedIn, your profile is how you present yourself to the world, and first impressions are important. Yes, you are a salesperson, but you are a person first. Present yourself in a friendly manner. Use a smiling headshot.

In the "Info" section of your profile, there are the following subsections:

- Education and Work
- Philosophy
- Arts and Entertainment
- Activities and Interests
- Networks
- Basic Information
- Contact Information

We suggest that you populate these sections as fully as you can. By creating a robust Facebook profile, you're letting people know who you are and also opening up sales opportunities.

List the relevant basics: where you went to school, where you work and where you used to work, what kind of music and movies you like, and what kind of activities you enjoy. Be generous in providing other relevant information about yourself. After all, you are painting a picture of who you are, and you are also more likely to find other people with similar interests.

In your Info section, you should include links to where you work, links to your LinkedIn profile, and links to your Twitter account. Also include your contact information. Be accessible. You can always change this information in the future if you choose to, but keep in mind that the more ways that people have to connect with you, the more ways in which you can positively influence them.

## Your Facebook Wall

Once you have created your profile, you will immediately start interacting with your friends on Facebook. You do this primarily by posting things on your wall. This is the main feature of your profile page. It is essentially a mosaic of who you are and what you are interested in. Here, you can post a mix of things that are related to what you enjoy doing and give your business contacts an opportunity to see the real "you." There are no limits to what you post: the content could be a list of brands that you admire or products that you recommend, links to interesting articles on websites, funny pictures that are appropriate, or almost anything, really. You're limited only by your imagination.

By observing what someone else posts on her wall, you can gain an amazing insight into the person. Now, we realize that we're playing armchair psychologists here, but little things are indicators of bigger things. And by logging in to Facebook and pulling up your news feed, you'll see a never-ending flow of things that your business contacts are posting, people that they're connecting with, events that they're promoting, and many other pieces of information.

By clicking on the names of those who are posting comments, you can see their full profiles. You can also see their information pages and the pictures that they have posted in their photo albums. Again, we have to emphasize that we are not talking about stalking here. We are all learning that we live in a more and more open society, and sharing information through sites like Facebook is fast becoming the new norm.

## News at the Speed of Light

A point that we have reiterated several times in this book bears mentioning again here: as you are learning about people, remember that, all things being equal, people do business with and refer business to people whom they know, like, and trust. And by building relationships with your business contacts on Facebook, you will increase the number of know-like-trust relationships that you have. Never approach this from a manipulative or sneaky perspective. You may think, "Well, I'll just become friends with all my prospects, and they will never know that I am going to be trying to sell them something." Wrong. People aren't stupid. We all know when we are dealing with insincere individuals who have a hidden agenda.

Also remember that what goes around comes around. If social networking is enabling us to share information literally at the speed of light, that means that good information and bad information can travel extremely quickly. If you develop a reputation for being sneaky and manipulative, you will quickly be ignored on a mass scale. Once you make a business faux pas on Facebook, it has a tendency to stay with you. And we mean for a long time!

The fact is that the days of the stereotypical salesperson who treats other people (prospects, clients, referral partners, and so on) like commodities and gets away with it because no one else knows about it are over. Without getting too philosophical here, it serves us all very well to be aboveboard in everything that we do. People are going to figure us out sooner or later. And you can't outrun your reputation. Ever hear of Tiger Woods or Bret

Favre? What do you think of first when you hear those names? Golf? Football? Or something else?

On a related note, whenever you are participating in social networking on Facebook, don't post anything that you consider too controversial without realizing that you may offend some people. We're not promoting political correctness in all areas of your business actions; however, using good taste is just good common sense.

# Groups

Facebook Groups are a great way to connect with businesspeople who have interests similar to yours and, by definition, people who may fit your targeted sales demographic. You will also encounter people who have problems that you can solve. As with LinkedIn, we suggest starting a group around any topic or idea that is relevant to your area of expertise and/or your industry.

The easiest way to do this is to think about what you do or what your company does in terms of solving a problem and build your group around that topic. By using this approach, you are automatically positioning yourself as a thought leader and an expert. Invite your clients and business friends who you feel would find value by joining your group. You're building a community. It's all about adding value.

As with other aspects of your Facebook activity, never introduce selling efforts into your group. There is a time and a place for straight-up selling on Facebook, and it is called fan pages. We will discuss these in more detail later in this chapter. Use your group as a place to create dialogue, share information, and collaborate. One great attention-getter here is to post video clips that you know your group will find interesting. You can conduct searches through YouTube and quickly find videos on almost any subject. From that point, it's easy: copy the link from YouTube into your group and post your thoughts on the matter. Ask for people's feedback. Great conversations can begin from there.

When you have created a group on Facebook, you will see that there is a section called "Discussions." This is a wonderful place to post thoughts, ideas, and questions and create dialogue. Here, you can track conversations and generate great value for the members of your group. Many people think that when it comes to groups, size matters—that you have to build a monstrous group with tons of members to have it be relevant. That's not necessarily the case. Yes, it's nice to have a large group with lots of activity, but you may be surprised at how much even a smaller community of people can get out of a group. The most important issues are what topics are introduced for discussion and how active the participants are. Irrespective of the number of people that participate, it is worth mentioning that when people join your group, you can send messages to them directly. The messages that you send them will go directly to their in-boxes.

Here are a few ways in which you can generate interest in your group:

- *Let people know about your group.* Go to www.godaddy.com, purchase a domain name for your group, and put the domain name on your business cards, your website (if you have one), your LinkedIn profile, and your e-mail signature. It makes no sense to take the time to create a group and not let as many people as possible know about it.

- *Run interesting contests and promotions in your group.* People get interested and engaged when there is some kind of a prize or contest going on.
- *Allow someone else to join you as an administrator for your group.* This frees you up a bit and gives others the chance to be more involved. That person will also be promoting the group to his friends and to all the folks that he interacts with on other social networking platforms.
- *Share the link to your group in your personal profile.* This should be in the same area as your contact information.
- *Let everyone on each of your social networking platforms know about your group.* This creates cross-pollination and leads to more interaction among the people you communicate with. You're a giver, not a taker.

# Fan Pages

Facebook Fan Pages are designed for use by businesses. Whereas a group tends to create a smaller community of like-minded people, a fan page is a public forum for reaching lots of people. The company that you sell for may already have a fan page. Unless you are self-employed or a business owner, you are probably not going to want to create your own fan page.

You can customize fan pages in lots of ways, and there are many people and companies that will sell you customizable packages to make creating a unique fan page easier. As time goes by, people are figuring out ways to build engaging fan pages without having to pay a Web developer a lot of money to do so. As an added benefit, fan pages are also indexed by Google, so anyone searching Google can potentially learn about your fan page.

Unlike groups, fan pages are about promotion. On your fan page, there is nothing wrong with letting people know that you have a product or service to provide. However, that does not mean that your fan page wall should be a nonstop sales pitch. It is certainly reasonable for you to provide information regarding your product or service and post interesting information that your fans see value in. If you limit your fan page information to this level of content, though, the result you will get is having visitors "like" your page but, in most cases, never return. (When you like something on Facebook or elsewhere online, you have the opportunity to click the "Like" button, which then broadcasts to your Facebook friends the fact that you like whatever it is. A great way to measure favorable opinion of a product or an idea is to see how many people "like" it.) Having a lot of fans who have "liked" your fan page but have no reason to return to it does you no good other than the ego rush of seeing the number of your fans.

When it comes to using Facebook effectively for business purposes, it's crucial that you create a customized landing page for your fan page. This is like an online billboard; it is the image that a person sees when she comes to your fan page for the first time. You should welcome her and let her know about the value that she will receive by becoming a fan. You can add video here, and you should. What could be better than a potential fan being greeted by your smiling face and your extending your online hand in friendship? Additionally, on your landing page, you should also have links to your LinkedIn and Twitter profiles. As we've said before, you should be connecting with your potential customers across as many platforms as you can.

There are many ways in which you can customize your fan page, including adding links to photos, videos, discussions, polls, events, notes, blogs, YouTube, and SlideShare, among many others. Be creative and try your hand at using these applications. All of them provide opportunities for you to deliver content that will engage people and have them wanting to know more about you and your company.

Another important function that you should utilize on your fan page is the "Resources" area. Post information here that people who visit your fan page can use immediately. Don't be afraid to give away value-based information or ideas. The old days of nickel-and-diming people for the purchase of knowledge have no place in the social networking world. In fact, if you operate that way, you serve only to commoditize yourself—and value generators are not commodities. With regard to providing value, it is also important for you to update the information on your fan page regularly, as this will keep people interested in returning.

## Facebook Ads

The shift in advertising spending from traditional mass media like newspapers, television, and radio to online advertising is the result of one significant liability that is inherent in all traditional media: when you advertise there, the great majority of the people who see your message have no interest whatsoever in what you are offering. You are essentially throwing away a lot of money on wasted exposures, hoping to generate enough revenue from a much smaller core group of buyers to justify the investment. In the past, advertisers just accepted this as a cost of getting their message out, and the effectiveness of this effort often did provide an acceptable return on their investment.

Let's revisit the fact that all social networking sites are databases at their core. The Big Brother aspect notwithstanding, more and more information on humans and their likes, dislikes, habits, and millions of other different statistics is now being aggregated on social networking sites. This is very powerful information. Social media are sometimes referred to as the world's largest sociology experiment. Until we had the tools that the Internet and social media provide, we did not have the ability to get extremely granular in terms of targeted advertising. The result is that today there are a number of online resources that allow you to be laser-like in terms of whom you place your message in front of when you are advertising. Facebook is one of those resources.

Everything that people are putting into their profiles and posting on their Facebook walls is being fed into server farms. That's a lot of data. Revisit the statistics that we gave at the beginning of this chapter and realize that those numbers are growing daily. Now put on your marketing hat. Imagine if you could selectively target exactly those people that you would like to present with an ad for your goods or services based on their self-identified statistics. Welcome to Facebook Ads.

These are the messages that appear on the right-hand side of almost every page on Facebook. They are very small, taking up only a tiny fraction of your page, but size is irrelevant here. Because of the targeting capability, they can be very powerful.

In fact, most people have no idea just how powerful these ads are—the average Facebook browser dismisses them as unimportant. This is not a tool to be underestimated, though. When you click on one of these ads, you are redirected to whatever website (or fan page) the creator of the ad wants you to see. Best of all, until someone clicks on the ad, it hasn't cost the creator of the ad a single penny. Nothing. You pay only for clicks here, not views.

Now let's use an odd example to prove an interesting point. Imagine that your company has the very specific target demographic of females from 21 to 40 years old who like Mötley Crüe and Nascar and who live within 20 miles of your home. Back in the old days, this would have been a tricky marketing problem, requiring months of research. Today, it would take you about five minutes to create such an ad, and the only people who would ever see it would be females from 21 to 40 years old who like Mötley Crüe and Nascar and who live within 20 miles of your home. The days of intrusive, interruptive ads that you have no interest in are coming to an end. It's just that many companies and their salespeople haven't gotten the message yet. Now you have.

## Creating the Ad

If advertising is the equivalent of throwing mud at the wall, at least make sure that you're throwing it at the right wall (that would be the "wall" feature on Facebook, of course). When you click on "Create an Ad" above the ads on the right-hand side of your page, Facebook will take you through a simple three-step process. You'll be asked to come up with the headline and the wording, and you have a very limited number of characters that you can use. The ad is small, so there is no room for a long spiel. Therefore, your message needs to be short and sweet. You can also upload a picture. Facebook will then ask you for the demographics of the people you would like the ad to be seen by: males, females, age groups, geographic destinations, and so on. Once you have provided this information, you can put in keywords to further refine your targeted demographic. Facebook will then ask where you would like people to be redirected to when they click on your ad.

The payment system, like those for most online advertising resources, operates basically as an auction. Facebook will tell you what the ad will cost you for every person who clicks on it. As of this writing, the clicks are in the 50 cents to a dollar range. You can also let Facebook know what your budget is, which can be as little as $10 per day. So let's say you create an ad and, just to use round numbers, let's say that Facebook says that you'll be charged 50 cents for every click. You tell Facebook that your budget is $10 per day. And let's also assume that people start clicking on your ad when it shows up on their Facebook pages. Now remember, the only people whose Facebook pages your ad is showing up on are the people who fit the exact parameters that you chose when you created the ad. Once 20 people have clicked on your ad (at 50 cents per click), the ad shuts off until 12:01 a.m. the next morning.

Your budget will never get blown out, because you have told Facebook exactly what your budget is. Your advertisement isn't showing up on the page of someone who doesn't fit your targeted demographic because you told Facebook what your targeted demographic is. And because you created the ad, you have the ability to log in to your account and see some great demographic data. Facebook won't tell you the exact identity of the people who clicked on your ad, but it will tell you things like male-to-female ratio, zip codes, and other information related to those people. Again, marketing people (and savvy salespeople) can learn a lot from this information. You can really track the effectiveness of your advertising and adjust or modify your message as you go along. By measuring which ads appealed to which sectors of people, you will know how to focus your next ad to reach that same group again (or avoid it, if the ad was appealing to the wrong demographic).

Recently, we were delivering a presentation to a group of CEOs in Dallas, and we started explaining the functionality of Facebook Ads and how the technology could help these executives to increase the visibility of their businesses. One of the participants told a quick story about a plastic surgeon friend of his. He shared that the plastic surgeon had learned about Facebook Ads and was skeptical (as most people are), but he had decided to give it a try. He went through the steps outlined here, taking a few minutes to create an ad based on his demographic target.

We asked the CEO to share the results of his doctor friend's marketing effort with Facebook. The CEO said, "You wouldn't believe it. Over six months, the surgeon's business grew by 30 percent!" These aren't fantasy figures. They are real, and they represent real results. Even if Facebook Ads go up to $10 a click, they will probably still be the cheapest advertising you will ever utilize because of the laserlike ability to target your demographic. Give it a shot. What do you have to lose? Maybe $10 a day. That's no more than some salespeople spend on coffee and doughnuts on a daily basis. And you can stop running the ad any time you want—probably when you cannot handle any more new business.

## Summary

Facebook is a juggernaut and a phenomenon. No one has exactly discovered the Rosetta stone yet on how to leverage Facebook for massive sales, but as we have demonstrated in this chapter, there are many ways to use Facebook for sales based on your business model. So in conclusion, let's cover a few reasons why you should be using Facebook for your business:

- It's the largest online community in the world, and will be for the foreseeable future. Since it has more than 500 million and is growing by more than one new user per second, you can't afford to ignore Facebook.
- By posting interesting content on your wall, you keep your name in front of your prospects, clients, and potential clients. But go easy on the sales pitches.
- As people engage with you on Facebook, both personally and on your fan page, you increase your brand. And this is something that follows you wherever you go, regardless of your employer. The best salespeople know that they are in the relationship business.
- Your friends and fans have friends. The average person on Facebook has 140 friends. And when people are active on Facebook, their actions often have a ripple effect. When you engage people, other people will become aware of you and your business organically.

- Communicating frequently with your friends and fans strengthens your relationships with them and gives you the ability to see whether your relationships are growing stronger.
- By using keywords strategically, you increase your visibility on major search engines, since Facebook is indexed by all major search engines.

Think about the time you spend on this platform in terms of marketing rather than direct selling. As we mentioned, the netiquette here is different from that on other social networking platforms, because this one is the most social of the bunch, so participate appropriately. Facebook is about creating, maintaining, and enhancing relationships with people. Keep it fun, stay updated, and people will want to interact with you and your company.

# CHAPTER 5

# BLOGGING IS EASIER THAN YOU THINK

## It's Also Worth the Effort

B ack in the days when dinosaurs roamed the earth (you know, late in the past century), the Internet was invented. In its early years of widespread use, from around 1995 to 2005, it was for the most part a read-only medium. Folks would log on (does anyone remember dial-up?), search sites like eBay and Amazon, get their news from sites like the Drudge Report, and basically surf in passive mode. That started changing for some people in the late 1990s and for most people by around 2005. The Internet went from what we refer to as a read-only environment to a read/write environment. And when the write aspect of the environment became established, well, that's when everything changed.

## What Is Blogging?

Social media are often associated with blogging. Anyone who is thinking of blogging only in terms of social media is really missing the boat, though. To explain what we mean by that, let's start from the beginning and define "blogging." A *blog* (short for "Web log") is basically a journal that exists online. It is a regularly updated account of events or ideas to which other people can add comments. At first, the computer nerds seemed to be the only ones writing blogs; over time, however, regular people like you started figuring out that you did not have to be a geek to have a blog.

Blogging started slowly increasing in popularity, and over time it has picked up momentum with incredible speed. As of this writing, according to Technorati, there are more than 120 million blogs, and more than 55,000 new ones are created every day. Now, since in some ways the Internet is the world's largest electronic bulletin board, some of these blogs are just spam. The vast majority of blogs will never have more than a few viewers, if they have any at all. Some people don't start a blog with the intention of becoming the next big thing, but rather just to have a place to post their thoughts.

Don't be intimidated by all these statistics; the numbers are misleading, just like the number of health club memberships. Hypothetically, your local gym has a limited number of memberships available, based on the limited amount of floor space and exercise equipment that it has. The reason that your health club can sell so many more memberships than it has space for members is that just because someone joins a gym does not necessarily mean that he is going to work out on a regular basis. And, just because someone starts a blog does not mean that she is going to be updating it and using it as the great communication tool that it is. In fact, in most cases, it is quite the reverse. According to Technorati, of the 120 million blogs on the Internet, only 7.4 million were updated in the past 90 days.

If you want to get real value from blogging, you cannot be the equivalent of one of those people whose Bowflex machine has become a very expensive clothes hanger in the corner of his bedroom. You are not starting a blog on a whim for no reason, and then letting it wilt, unread, in some corner of the Internet. You're going to have a purpose and commit to using your blog to its fullest potential. That is what professionals bring to blogging, and it's why professional salespeople make the big bucks.

## Why Blog?

There is some controversy in the sales world as to whether salespeople should be blogging at all, and some of that controversy is well founded and worth reviewing.

At the time of this writing, there is a huge void when it comes to the governance of employee activity on the Internet. You need to remember that, in the blogging world, most companies do not currently have an editing department to review what you write and approve it before it is out there. What this means to you is that any activities that you conduct online as a representative of your company, and, more pointedly, anything that you say, can reflect on your employer in ways that your employer may find objectionable. In Chapter 7, we talk at length about netiquette and about the importance of using good judgment about what you put out there, but in that chapter, the point is primarily about having good online manners.

In this chapter, however, we are talking about the issue of potentially damaging your company's brand, its relationships with its customers, and its standing in the marketplace, and even exposing yourself and your employer to liability issues. Nowhere is the potential for bad judgment, and resultant damages, more prevalent than it is with blogging.

So here is the bottom line: we strongly recommend that you do not write a business blog as a representative of your company without gaining your employer's approval first. We also strongly recommend that all companies with employees prepare and implement a policy on the posting of Internet content that includes a filtering and approval process, so that no member of the company's workforce posts potentially damaging content. This issue is in its infancy, but at the same time it is an important issue that you will most likely be hearing a lot more about as this area develops.

Some salespeople think that blogging is pointless and a waste of their valuable selling time. In some instances, this view may be correct. For example, if you're working for a Fortune 500 company, it's more than likely that the company already has a blog, or maybe multiple blogs. If it doesn't, shame on it. Put down this book, call your marketing department, and tell it to get on the ball. Pronto.

Yes, in an enterprise business, blogging should be one of the essential functions of the marketing department. The marketing gurus should be creating a river of content regarding your products and services, how they help your prospects, and relevant conversations, experiences, and dialogues. Ideally, marketing departments should always be creating opportunities for us to sell through many different ventures, including blogging. But what if you don't have a marketing department?

At this point in time, according to the U.S Census Bureau, more than 75 percent of all the businesses in America are considered small to midsized businesses. Most of these businesses do not have marketing departments. Maybe they have someone wearing multiple hats, one of which is a quasi-marketing role, but in this economy, most companies are running lean and mean. We have worked for companies where the sales and marketing roles were rolled into one. In a small to midsized business, there may be some validity in farming out some of the blogging to an inexpensive freelance copywriter. Again, every business will have a different budget for this, if any. The onus of blogging may then fall squarely on your shoulders.

So, why bother starting a blog? The simple answer is, because it is easy. You know a great deal about your industry, how you serve it, and what your prospects and clients are looking for. Your blog is another avenue for you to become the value generator that the modern professional salesperson needs to be in order to gain new business.

Another important reason to start your blog is that that's what thought leaders do. By not having a blog, you are diminishing your opportunity to establish yourself as a thought leader or someone who is thought of as a value generator. In every industry, including yours, there are people like you who are blogging. You may be thinking, "I'm no writer," but you're not trying to become Herman Melville here. You can be conversant, can't you? Writing is just speaking on paper, or on the Web. Let's not over-complicate things. A salesperson should always be commenting on things that are of interest to her prospects anyway—this is just doing that online. You shouldn't be spending a lot of time doing so, but you need to join the party.

The main reason for blogging is that you have something to say to the world. You have all this information and all these thoughts and ideas that come into your mind every day. You have specialization and keen insight into your area, and you need to get it out somehow; you also need to incorporate what others are saying. Effective selling, after all, is about listening. By having a blog, you're sharing your valuable content with the world, and then you are listening very closely for replies. Isn't that what conversation is all about? And aren't the best salespeople also the best conversationalists? In our experience, that tends to be the case, by necessity.

# Getting Started

The most common thing people that ask themselves when they decide to start blogging is, "How do I set it up, and what do I write about?" We'll get into the nitty-gritty of actually setting up your blog later in the chapter, but first let's focus on the content question. Believe it or not, from time to time, there's actually nothing wrong with writing about your favorite sports teams, your kids, your hobbies, or anything else you're interested in but you have to be careful about how you do it. As someone who's looking to grow his sales numbers, you are going to have to be strategic about your content.

You're looking to position yourself as an expert in your field, which means that as you're posting content, you should consistently be writing on a theme that is relevant to your business interests. You can occasionally write things that are non-business in nature, as previously mentioned, but just make sure that when people are coming to your blog, they can figure out pretty quickly which area you are an expert in. Keep a balance between the personal stuff and the business stuff, and skew it toward business.

Write about the aspects of your area that you're passionate about. You're passionate about your industry, right? (If not, why haven't you changed jobs yet?) Let that come through in your blogging. The things that you're passionate about will become a never-ending well of posts. The enthusiasm that you feel about those topics will also come through in your writing.

One of the interesting things about the evolution of the Internet is the niche factor in markets. Unlike with previous forms of mass media, we now have the ability to get very granular in specific subject areas. When we say granular, it doesn't mean that all you're going to write about is a particular widget. Not at all. You may sell that widget, but the widget is part of a larger industry. You should write about things that are relevant to people in the widget industry. Remember, you're positioning yourself as a thought leader in your industry, not as someone with a Ph.D. in widgets. As people read your posts, they'll figure out that you have the necessary knowledge of widgets to provide a valuable perspective on the matter. That's a given. What's not a given is that you serve the prospect's broader business interests. That's what value generators do.

If you're looking to grow your readership (and yes, you are), you should be posting updated content on a regular basis. We recommend that you post something at least once a week, and preferably once every business day. Doing so keeps people engaged and shows that your blog hasn't become a Bowflex in the corner with clothes on it. As in offline conversations, if there are large gaps between comments, the other person's interest wanes. It's your job to keep the conversation going.

If you want to steadily attract new readers in your industry, you should work hard at coming up with a clever title for your blog. If you just use your name, it will limit readers' ability to find you in all the online chatter. If you do use your name, use it as part of a short title—something that identifies the prominent theme of your content. Here are some blog names that demonstrate these principles: Creating Revenue and Retention, All Biz Answers, and Beyond the Boardroom.

## Blog Mechanics

Now that you have determined your primary theme and the title of your blog, it's time to walk through the process of technically creating a blog. The good news is that over the past five years or so, this has become easy. No pocket protector or tape on the glasses needed here. Here are three of the most popular blogging services.

### TypePad

TypePad (www.typepad.com) is a paid service that costs between about $5 a month to close to $100 a month. The company claims to have designed its blogging template for small businesses and professionals, and this shows in how clean and simple it is.

Because you're paying for the use of the service, advertising spam will not appear on your blog. TypePad also has better customer service than some of its competitors.

## Blogger

As Google continues to take over the universe, it is offering more services all the time, including blogging services. Like most things that Google offers, Blogger (www.blogger.com) is simple, and it's free. Starting a Blogger site requires that you have a Gmail account. Most folks already have a Gmail account, and if you don't, it's time you did. (There are plenty of examples throughout this book that should convince you that this is the case.)

Blogger is so user-friendly that you can have your blog up and running in no time. Google, like TypePad, also handles the server space. One thing that may concern you is that your blog address will be yourblog.blogspot.com. You will have to live with "blogspot" in your address. Although it's not as nice as having your own domain name, it's not a big deal, and it will work for your purposes.

## WordPress

Like some social networking sites, WordPress (www.wordpress .org; www.wordpress.com) runs on open-source code, which means that there is a large community of coders who are writing programs that integrate with WordPress. The more commonly known version of WordPress is the dot-org version. With this version, you download the software and host the blog on your site. If you're like most salespeople, however, you don't have your own website, so the dot-com version may be better suited for you. The dot-com version is hosted, and it is also free. I think we can all agree that free is always good, but even more so in a post-recession economy!

Personally, we each run our respective blogs on WordPress. Neither of us is a computer geek. We understand that using computers is a fact of life nowadays, but we have no intention of becoming computer experts. After all, just because we drive cars doesn't mean that we feel the need to learn how to rebuild a transmission. WordPress is probably the most user-friendly of the options discussed here, and when we have questions about it, there are lots of online tutorials, YouTube videos, and blogs on WordPress itself that can help noncomputer experts like us. If you want something fixed regarding a website, or your computer, you can also do what we do: give your computer to a 13-year-old. It'll be fixed in minutes.

One of the reasons we love WordPress is that there are so many ways in which you can customize your blog. You can choose from many templates. Don't feel that you have to pay someone to create a whizbang template design for you. Most templates are great right out of the box. Pick a template that's pleasant looking, and don't try to create a *Mona Lisa*. Simply provide a clean header, which is what shows at the top of every page, in case someone wanders into your blog by accident. Let her know immediately where she is.

## Initial Blog Posting Concerns

Use a short, catchy blog title for every post. As with most things, you'll get better at this as time goes by. You'll want to keep your titles short and sweet, though. Most people are in a hurry, and if your post's title doesn't catch their attention, they won't stop to read it. You're in sales, so you know the importance of getting people's attention quickly. Many salespeople are familiar with the concept of the elevator pitch. This is the idea that you have only as much time with your prospect as it takes to ride a few floors in an elevator, so how can you describe what you do for a living or what your product or service does in a way would be important to your prospect? Take that general concept and apply it to your blog posts' titles. Grab your readers quickly.

You can have your blog list the date and time when each of your posts was created. This is a good idea because it shows people the frequency of your blogging. There's also a bio section on your blog. Use this area to explain who you are, what you do, and the value you bring to the marketplace. Don't use this area as a sales pitch. As in your LinkedIn profile, paint an accurate word picture that portrays you in the best possible light. Make sure you use a smiling headshot. It's all about approachability, right? Be friendly, and put your best foot forward.

Tags are labels that you add to your posts that allow the posts to be filed in categories that you create. These are related to the different subject areas you'll be blogging about. As time goes by, you may find yourself creating more tags than you initially set out to. That's a good thing. We certainly have ended up finding new areas within our respective industries that we have been able to mine for fresh content. As you write more posts, the number of things you write about will grow, and this is normal. As the number of subjects grows, your list of tags will also grow. And when people are looking at your blog, they can very easily click on whatever subject areas (tags) they feel they would have the most interest in. You can even turn on a functionality that indicates how many posts there are in each category. This, of course, will allow people to see very quickly, right from your home page, what subjects you're blogging about the most and where your expertise lies.

There are many other areas of your blog that you can modify, including the display of pictures and other such material. Depending on which blog service you use, the functions available may be slightly different, and more are added all the time. Just understand the principles behind your blog functions and use the appropriate tools as you see fit.

Of course, one of your goals is to have people reading your blog frequently, and one way to accomplish this is through links. We are big believers in and promoters of paying it forward. Just as we discussed "liking" people's posts on Facebook, commenting on people's status updates on LinkedIn, and retweeting people's tweets on Twitter, adding links in your blog posts is a huge pay-it-forward activity.

## Linking

If you're mentioning specific information that you read about somewhere else or discussing someone else's work or ideas, you should be giving credit where credit is due. It's just the right thing to do, and what goes around comes around. By adding a link to the other person's blog or website, you will come across his radar, and that presents an opportunity for you to build a relationship with him. This way, whomever you've linked to might link back to you when you have an interesting post that is up his alley. It also shows the world that you respect other people and that you're not trying to be the be-all and end-all. Share the spotlight.

Including the link is easy. On your blog dashboard (where you write your blog posts before posting them), you'll see a button that you can click on to insert a link. When you use this button, the link will show up as a different color, and people will know that they can click on it.

Now, you would never insincerely add links to try to suck up, would you? Nah. But by sincerely paying it forward, you may be in a position to gain a lot of readers. Let's say that you add a link to a famous blogger who has a tremendous number of readers. Some blogs even have software that displays the number of people who have subscribed and are notified every time the blogger adds a new post. And remember, when you provide links to another blogger, that blogger usually adds a link back to you. Your blog has now become visible to all the people who are reading the other person's blog. We've seen instances in which people have increased their readers by hundreds, if not thousands, of people in a single day. Don't spend a lot of time trying to gain a bajillion readers, though. Just follow good netiquette and pay it forward, and your readership will grow over time. Every once in a while you may get a big bump in readers, but don't waste any effort trying to rig the system. What goes around comes around. As with exercise, small activities repeated over time produce amazing results.

## Drawing a Crowd

Now that you're on your way, let's talk about how to gain readers. Taking the time to create content and position yourself as a value generator pays off by having people read your blog and spread the word about you.

In the beginning, it may feel as if you're putting in a lot of work and not getting a lot of traction. This is normal. It's rather like working out. You're probably going to exercise and get sore for a while before you start to notice any results. People who tell you that you're going to see life-changing results from anything immediately are usually just trying to get to your wallet. Grownups know that things take time. Put in the work. Pay your dues. These are clichés because they're true.

Let people know that you now have a blog. Of course, at first the only people you're going to be telling this to are probably your friends, your family, and your coworkers. On your blog, you can add an RSS feed, which is a way of alerting people that you've just posted something new. You can also add a widget that e-mails people whenever you post something. Depending on which blog service you're using, you'll see how to add these links and widgets. It's easy.

Here are a few ways to get the word out.

## Your Newsletter

Do you have a newsletter yet? If so, you'll want to mention that you have a blog and add a link to it. Let people know what the main theme of your blog is, and start to build buzz around your blog. If you don't have a newsletter, get ready to learn more about why you should have one and how to implement it in Chapter 6.

## LinkedIn

In your LinkedIn profile, you have the ability to add up to three website links. One of these links should be to your blog. And make sure that you label it "My Blog" so that people can clearly see that it's a link to your blog. You should also add the Word-Press or TypePad application to your LinkedIn profile. This application shows a shortened version of your blog right on your profile, and when people click on it, it opens a new Web page on their computer. And guess what Web page that is . . . drum roll, please . . . that's right, it's your blog.

## Facebook

Facebook has an application called Networked Blogs. When you activate this application, whenever you post something on your blog, it automatically also posts to your Facebook page. Now you're spreading your message across multiple platforms at the same time. And as for the new people who are becoming fans of your Facebook fan page, they will see the link in your customized landing page, indicating that they may also want to sign up for your blog. Now that's smart time management!

## Twitter

As with Facebook, you can add a widget to your blog so that whenever you add a post, a tweet will go out saying something like, "Here's my most recent blog post," with a link to it. You're cooking with gas now, you social media maven!

## E-mail

You should always be adding links to your social networking sites and your blog in the contact information section of your e-mail signature. When you do this, any time someone receives an e-mail from you, you are promoting your various social networking profiles and your blog. Make sure to say something in the e-mail signature like, "Let's connect on LinkedIn, Facebook, Twitter, or my blog at," and then add the links to each of those sites. Talk about killing a bunch of birds with one stone, huh?!

## Search Engines

You may find this hard to believe, but there are people who are looking for you. Maybe they're not looking for you specifically (yet), but they're looking for people who know what you know. That's called being a thought leader and a value generator. If you were looking for something, you'd probably go to Google and type in a keyword. That's what people are also doing when they're looking for you. So realize that the keywords in your blog posts are being indexed by Google, Yahoo!, MSN, and all the other major search engines. The way that some companies and individuals try to beef up the presence of certain keywords in Google searches is a process known as SEO, or search engine optimization.

You shouldn't add keywords to your posts in awkward places or too frequently, but always keep in the back of your mind that all your content is being scanned by search engines. Using certain keywords repeatedly (and you will be doing this automatically, since your blog has a major theme) will raise your rankings in search results. Don't go spending a ton of money on some SEO expert to guarantee you first-page ranking on Google. Just write compelling content that is rich in keywords and let the search engines do what they do naturally.

## Blogrolls

Blogrolls are links on your blog that show others whom you follow and, by extension, whom you consider to be thought leaders. This is a huge way to pay it forward. Again, always be sincere and transparent. If you add a blogroll, send a message to the person whose blog you've listed on your blogroll letting her know that you've done so. Don't demand or expect that she will do so for you in return. By adding links to another person's blog from time to time in an appropriate, natural fashion, you will get her attention. Use your great relational and networking skills and see whether, over time, you're being added to others' blogrolls. The world is getting smaller. Pay it forward.

Of course, as we will discuss in the next chapter, you should have a Google Reader account, and as we mentioned in Chapter 3, you should have Google Alerts on your name, your company name, and other keywords that are important for you to monitor. By having a Google Alert set up related to your blog, you'll know immediately every time someone mentions your blog.

## Pressing the Flesh

With all this talk of the Internet and social media, let's not forget some of the old-school ways of doing things. Does anyone remember a time before cell phones and the Internet? In the old days, the way you let people know about things was that you told them. Sometimes we find ourselves staring at our BlackBerrys and iPhones so much that we forget that we're interacting with people all the time. In every meeting and at every appointment, you should mention that you have a blog. Remember that people are always most interested in what's important to them, so make sure you phrase it in such a way that there's value to them in knowing that you have a blog. Let them know that you're seeking to be a value generator for them. Yes, it's fine to actually tell them that. All things being equal, people do business with and refer business to people that they know, like, and trust. Being genuinely, disarmingly honest with people is one of the fastest ways to develop a know-like-trust relationship.

Ask people if it's okay for you to send them a link to your blog. When you get back to your computer, send them a thank-you e-mail for meeting with you (you are doing this, right?) and include a link to your blog. Let the person know that he can sign up to have your blog posts e-mailed to him for his convenience instead of his having to keep going back to your blog to see if you've posted anything new. Make it easy for people. And let them know that if you're ever in a position to drive business their way, you certainly will.

# Earn Your Blogging Black Belt

Let's wrap up by discussing how to write. No, not how to actually push the keys on your keyboard, but how to provide content and generate value without looking as if you're struggling to write. It's not your goal to win a Pulitzer with your blog. It's your goal to increase your sales. Here are eight tips to help you become a blogging black belt.

## 1. Blog Frequently

As with anything we do that we're serious about, we schedule time to do it in our calendar. Thinking that you'll get around to blogging sometime later in the week leads to never getting around to blogging. Things that are not scheduled have an annoying tendency not to get done. Blogging is like exercise. Figure out when during the week you're going to spend a little time writing, and just do it.

People will be checking your blog to see if there is new content there. By blogging frequently, you're piling up content so that when loyal readers return to your blog, there's something new for them to read, and when new viewers come to your blog, they can see that you've been busy. And all those posts add value to your readers. You're building a gold mine for them and for you.

## 2. Measure Your Metrics

As every manager knows, what isn't measured can't be modified. You're writing content and you're getting the word out, so it makes sense to check your results. Check your blog analytics on Google (google.com/analytics). Google offers visitor tracking and analysis reports. As with most things Google, you'll need a Gmail account, which, as we mentioned before, you should have by now. It's pretty simple to use Google's analytics and statistics display tools to determine how many people are visiting your blog. You can break the data down into hits, page views, visits, visitors, and other parameters. This is a techie's and a marketing person's dream. Don't go crazy with this information; just familiarize yourself with these tools and track your results.

## 3. Write Naturally

Sometimes people ask us how they should talk on social media sites. Hmm, that seems like the kind of question a schizophrenic might have. There's only one way to talk: be yourself! You already know how to blog—just the same way you speak. Don't start trying to come across as brighter than you are or as someone that you're not. Simply be yourself, because everyone else is already taken.

However you talk in real life is exactly the way you should sound on your blog. How could you not? Social media force transparency. We've all been fed the slick pitches long enough. People want authenticity. Give it to them. It'll be like a breath of fresh air.

If you really want to take us literally, pick up a voice-to-text software program that converts everything you say out loud into text on your computer in real time. You can sit in your office with a cup of coffee in your hand and just talk. Whatever you say will show up on your computer screen as you're saying it. It's actually the coolest thing you've ever seen the first time you try it. It's like a ghost is typing everything you're saying. When you're done, do a quick edit, and you're good to go. It even has a spell check, and once you've trained it to recognize your voice, it will automatically add punctuation. This should get you used to seeing your "voice" typed out on the screen.

Every top salesperson carries a digital voice recorder with her at all times in order to catch thoughts as they come. We often get our best thoughts when we're driving to or from an appointment. But you can't write while you're driving. So while you're driving, you can be speaking into your voice recorder so you can convert it to text later on. The old days of writing a book are now becoming the new days of speaking a book. I'm actually typing this on my keyboard right now because we both like typing, but if we wanted to, we could have spoken this entire book into existence. After a while, the training wheels will come off, and you'll be able to type in your voice just fine.

## 4. Interview Players in Your Industry

You know who the thought leaders and players in your industry are. When you're attending trade shows, networking meetings, association meetings, or anywhere else you'll bump into these people, interview them. If possible, ask them ahead of time if they'd be open to a brief interview. They will be flattered that you're interested in them. Pick up an inexpensive video flipcam and take it with you everywhere. Let the person know that you'd like to post the video on your blog. (Did we forget to mention that you can post video on your blog? Oh, yeah, you can do that—and you should!) Your flipcam can probably also just record audio if you or the other person prefers, and you can post that instead.

You're gathering tremendous content that can be reformatted across multiple social networking platforms and, of course, on your blog. This is wonderful exposure for the other person and helps positions you as the go-to person who's got his finger on the pulse on your industry. She is going to want to post that video on her own site, and that will automatically drive viewers to your site. Genius.

### 5. Comment on Other People's Blogs

Effective blogging is about interaction. Look at other people's blogs and post comments. If they've written something interesting, tell them so. At the least, thank them. Almost no one does this. Take the extra 30 seconds and write a comment on someone's blog saying that you appreciate the time he took to write his post.

In a more and more hurried world, it's the little niceties that people most often overlook. Not you, however—you're a professional. You know that niceties are the doors to relationships. As you comment on other people's blogs, you'll find that they'll start commenting on yours. You're starting to show up on their radar. Add constructive comments, and always remember what your mother told you: "If you don't have something nice to say, then don't say anything at all."

## 6. Be Helpful

Some people play their cards so close to their vest that they're basically turning people off with their coyness. We're now living in a very open world where people can very quickly learn all kinds of things that they didn't used to be able to find out easily. Give away your knowledge. We're not saying you should make dumb decisions here; we're saying you should share your wealth. And your wealth is your knowledge.

Sharing your knowledge with people will have them wanting to know you. You are a resource. You are a value generator. Try to include as much helpful information as you can on your blog. You never know who or where people are going to forward that information on to.

By not holding back and by adding massive value to your blog, you're letting people know a lot more about you than the fact that you know your stuff. You're letting people know that you value them and that you value relationships. Be helpful and be open.

## 7. Stay Focused

Keep your blog on point. You're going to be sharing a mix of personal and business-related things, but make sure that the personal doesn't overshadow the business. Remember the reason you started blogging—it was to grow your sales. Sometimes we forget obvious things, and we need to remind ourselves of them. Keep your posts on topic. Before you write, always think, "Will this have value for my readers?" If it takes you more than a few seconds to answer that, maybe you shouldn't be writing it. Stay relevant, stay focused, and stay top of mind to your prospects, your clients, and your referral sources.

## 8. Get In and Get Out

Keep your posts brief. We prefer to write posts that are no longer than 500 words, preferably 400 words. People are busy. They're looking for easily digestible information that is of value. If you write short, frequent posts, people will want to come back to your site and see what you're writing. When you write short posts that take no more than a few minutes to read, people will develop a comfort level with your writing style.

When you're writing short posts, you're not going to be continually putting undue pressure on yourself to come up with some brilliant content all the time for your blog. You'll be relaxed when it's your scheduled time to write (remember the scheduling tip?). As it relates to reading time, in the blogosphere, less is more. And the best conversationalists know that they are perceived as brilliant conversationalists when they say something briefly and then ask for feedback. That's the art of conversation and, ironically, also the art of sales.

## Summary

There was a time not that long ago when we had no choice but to accept information only from the mass media. We didn't question this game, because there was no alternative. As you well know by now, those days are long over. By learning how to use social media, including blogs, effectively, you can play a new game.

People are looking for help, and when you use the existing and up-and-coming tools, there has never been a better time to position yourself as the value generator that you are. It's a golden time to be a professional salesperson. You can identify and communicate with prospects in ways that previous generations of salespeople couldn't have imagined.

So once your employer has given you the go-ahead and you have an approval process in place for posting, you are ready to jump into the blog pool. It's really quite simple, and the ROI in terms of your market penetration, lead generation, business development, and branding potential is unlimited.

CHAPTER **6**

# ATTRACTING ATTENTION TO YOUR ONLINE PRESENCE

## How to Be a Magnet

As authors who make a living as speakers, we are approached regularly by vendors within our industry who try to persuade us to pay a fee to have our information included in a speaker directory. This type of marketing tool, created in both print and online versions, reads like an L.L.Bean catalog. It provides page after page of speaking professionals within our industry. It is usually sorted by area of expertise and includes the speaker's photo, a description of his topics, and his contact information. We both are included in these directories when the listings are provided free of charge. However, to date, neither of us has ever paid for this type of marketing, and it is highly unlikely that we ever will. The reason is simple: we understand how our buyers make hiring decisions when they are selecting a speaker. We know that our clients hire speakers whom they know, like, and trust, and we also know that blindly booking speakers from such directories is not part of that equation.

## Risk, Familiarity, and How Buyers Buy

In our line of work, meeting planners are our primary clients—the key buying contacts within the speaking business. Their customers, in turn, are the attendees who will be present at the conference or corporate meeting. Meeting planners are responsible for managing every aspect of a successful event, and they have an enormous task. They are involved in everything from selecting a conference theme, venue selection, menu planning, and event scheduling to designing and printing promotional materials, negotiating hotel rates, and creating name badges for the attendees. They also have the task of selecting speakers. When it comes to selecting a speaker, either they make the decision themselves or they submit their recommendation to a board of directors, which almost always approves the planners' selection. In any case, they are the focal point of the speaker selection process for the associations and corporations that employ them.

You might think that for a meeting planner, the nightmare scenario involving a speaker would be selecting one who does not show up as scheduled. Actually, that situation, although unwelcome, could turn out to be a blessing! After all, consider the alternative. That scenario would involve hiring a speaker who does show up—and who then bombs with her ensuing presentation to the audience. (Incidentally, this potential outcome is also why most people are more afraid of public speaking than of death!) For a meeting planner, the consequence of such a debacle is readily apparent: when the failed presentation concludes, the failed speaker shrugs, waves good-bye, and promptly heads for the airport. The meeting planner then stands alone for the duration of the conference, facing the five hundred or so unhappy attendees who just witnessed the carnage. He has to shoulder the blame for the presenter's poor skills because he was responsible for making what will be viewed by everyone at the conference as a poor hiring decision.

Which brings us back to understanding your customer's buying process. Like most buyers, meeting planners are risk-averse when they are making a purchase decision—in this case, hiring a speaker. Picking someone that they know nothing about out of a directory of speakers is the riskiest selection method available, and therefore it is both the least desirable and the least utilized. To avoid making a bad decision, they are better served by relying on someone else's recommendation.

In fact, the need for outside expertise as a risk-reduction tool in the speaker selection process is so significant that an entire industry exists for the sole purpose of alleviating it. Speakers' bureaus are the middlemen of the speaking profession. They provide meeting planners with a knowledgeable resource for finding high-quality presenters, and they exist primarily to mitigate the risk involved in selecting a speaker. These businesses maintain a stable of experts on a range of different topics, and they provide their expertise in the form of speaker recommendations based on the bureau's knowledge of its speaker partners and the meeting planner's event needs. They succeed in our business based on maintaining a reputation for providing consistently good product (presenters) to their meeting-planner clients, and they are paid out of the speaker's fee, usually in the form of a commission. Speakers' bureaus benefit both parties in the transaction. They provide the speaker with the benefit of getting hired, and they provide the meeting planner with the benefit of risk aversion. They also provide an added benefit to the meeting planner in the form of a bridge of familiarity between the speaker and the buyer. They facilitate buying based on the principle of know, like, and trust when this prerequisite does not exist.

As a salesperson, you have the same lack of know, like, and trust with new prospects that we as speakers do. Like us, you are one of a multitude of people who sell a similar product or service. You are an unknown entity to many potential buyers, none of whom is going to blindly select you, any more than a meeting planner is going to blindly select one of us. Here again, this is why cold-calling on people who do not know you is such an inefficient way to develop new leads: the resistance you encounter isn't nearly so much that the buyer does not have a need for what you sell as it is that she just does not know you.

Unfortunately, there is no "salespersons' bureau" to act as a bridge between you and your prospects. You will therefore need to do the bridge building of know, like, and trust yourself. Fortunately, social networking provides us with the means to do exactly that—and, best of all, you don't have to pay someone else a commission to receive the benefit.

## Delivering Value: Old Versus New

Although your business card may identify you as a salesperson, in the selling revolution, your job is not so much to "sell" as it is to provide consistent, ongoing value to your customers. You already know that the reason any business exists is to fill needs and solve the problems of its market. In your traditional role as a salesperson, you have accomplished this goal by providing goods and services to your customers based on their needs for what you sell. This is also how customers have traditionally defined the value proposition of a salesperson.

The problem that is inherent in the traditional selling model is that the benefit to the customer from working with you is largely limited to what occurs during the transaction process. In other words, in the past, your value to the marketplace has been largely limited to those times when a buyer or prospective buyer has an immediate need for what you sell. (Yes, you may consider "farming," or client relationship management, a part of your adding value, but let's face it: a lot of that posttransaction face time is of little real value to most customers, right?) Your opportunity to provide value has historically revolved around these purchasing episodes, and in each case, when the transaction is completed, your ability to provide personal value largely evaporates once the purchase order is signed or the contract is finalized.

In the Social Media Sales Revolution, that restriction on salespeople no longer applies. The technological phenomenon of social media as it pertains to adding value is this: it allows you to expand the fundamental purpose of a salesperson—to solve the needs and problems of his customers—far beyond the traditional transactional model. It allows you to deliver personal value outside the bounds of simple business transactions. It gives you the means to efficiently provide value to potential customers when they are not in the market for what you sell. Also, it provides you with the opportunity to brand yourself as a value generator within the business circles that you serve.

Why? Because while your prospects and customers do not always have a need for the products or services that you offer, they do have a continuous, never-ending need for useful information.

THE SOCIAL MEDIA SALES REVOLUTION

In today's world, of course, the vast majority of these people get that information via the Internet. They procure it in one of two fundamental ways: either they search for it themselves or it comes to them through resources that they follow with social media. If you can position yourself as one of those resources that they follow—specifically, an individual within your industry who provides useful information that solves its needs and problems—your market will follow you online, and you will accomplish three fundamentally important objectives as a value generator:

1. You will establish high-value relationships with both prospects and existing customers within the market(s) that you sell to.
2. You will eliminate transactional events as a prerequisite for delivering value to those whom you wish to do business with and instead will deliver value consistently.
3. You will reverse the relationship between seller and buyer. No longer will you be preoccupied with pursuing prospective customers. Instead, they will follow you.

Social media marketing is the vehicle that allows you to provide value to your market on a continual basis, even when you aren't involved in a transaction. This value is delivered in the form of content. Your role in this new selling environment is therefore to provide your prospects and customers with ongoing value by providing information (content) that solves their problems and addresses their needs.

By making sure that you communicate and add value online as much as possible, you build influence. Everything that you write essentially lives online somewhere forever. Even if only a small number of people find your information somehow, every little bit adds up. Once you get the hang of this, creating offline content in some ways almost seems obsolete.

# The Salesperson as Value Generator

We know what you are probably thinking as you consider the implications of this marketing shift. There are three major concerns with the concept that should be obvious to most busy salespeople who aren't knee-deep in social media already. First, "I'm not an expert." This is a common concern for people who feel that they cannot create ongoing "expertise" documents that their customers will find valuable on a continual basis. Second, "This sounds time-consuming." We're all busy, that's for sure, and it's easy to assume that you don't have the time available to do what it takes to be considered a value generator. Third, "I'm not a writer." This common concern prevents a lot of qualified people from providing content. All three points are worth discussing in detail, so let's take a closer look.

## Concern 1: "I'm Not an Expert"

You don't need to be an expert to provide consistent, worthy content. To illustrate, consider a common selling model. In the past, both of your authors have worked with distribution-based industries and their sales forces. There are many variations of this selling channel, but in almost all cases the relationships involve manufacturers that produce goods selling those goods through distributors; this is simply an alternative to selling them directly through an internally housed sales force. (Many manufacturers do both.) The distributors that represent a manufacturer are usually independent, privately owned businesses that are licensed to sell the manufacturer's goods and services in a defined territory. The distributor buys inventory from the manufacturer and then resells (distributes) it to customers within the distributor's defined markets.

As a value generator, your marketing process works in exactly the same way. The goods and services (content) that you provide to your online community (defined market) is "manufactured" by anyone and everyone on the Internet who is writing about information that is of interest. You get your "inventory" from these manufacturing sources (for free, of course), and then you distribute the best of that inventory to the customers and prospects who are following you within your online community.

Developing your business this way makes your role as a value generator to your online community that of a distributor of content and not, unless you choose to be one, a manufacturer of it. You will review relevant information online from those "manufacturers" that interest you, and your job will then be to evaluate this information, select items that are of interest to your followers, and, with a single click of your mouse, deliver it to every single one of them. The benefits to you are not only free but myriad and profound. By redistributing useful content to your online followers, you will build your own bridge of know, like, and trust with your online community. You will establish your brand as a thought leader and an expert. You will receive an invaluable free education in aspects of your industry from others in the business whose knowledge you do not currently possess. And, best of all, when the buyers—both existing customers and prospects—in your community have a need for what you sell, they are going to contact you because they buy, like all buyers do, based on familiarity. You are seen as the go-to source for value, and you are viewed as the option that presents the least risk.

## Concern 2: "This Sounds Time-Consuming"

Utilizing social media certainly would be time-consuming if we were suggesting that you spend hours on Google or one of the other search engines, continually typing in keywords and scouring the Internet for articles and information that would be useful to your online community. That is how you currently research information for yourself, right? And now you think that we are asking you to do the same thing for the benefit of your customers and prospects. Think again.

Let's go back to the distribution sales model for a moment. A distributor that sells for manufacturers does not go out into the marketplace every day looking for suppliers with products to sell. Rather, it has ongoing relationships with the manufacturers that it has chosen to work with, and those manufacturing partners supply the distributor with the products that it needs to provide to its end-user customers. The distributor doesn't have to go looking for inventory; inventory is provided to it by its selected manufacturing partners.

As a distributor of online content, you have the technology readily available to provide you with exactly the same kind of relationship, and service, that the traditional distributor gets from its manufacturers. With just a few simple steps on your computer, the online "manufacturers" (content producers) that you choose to partner with (follow) will deliver an endless supply of free, high-quality product (content) that you can then review and distribute to your end users as you see fit. In other words, after some initial setup work, no searching on your part is necessary; everything that you need will be delivered to your in-box the moment that it is produced.

### Concern 3: "I'm Not a Writer"

It's fine if you don't consider yourself a writer. As we just established, you don't have to be. But you should seriously consider becoming a writer of sorts by starting a blog of your own. Blogging affords you the opportunity to make a connection with your audience above and beyond your role as a distributor—to showcase your thoughts and opinions without restriction. We discussed your role as a blogger in the previous chapter.

## A Reminder . . .

In a moment we will look at the mechanics involved in making your social media marketing strategy a viable, functional reality. However, because you are a salesperson, before we do that it is important to revisit a point we made in Chapter 1 regarding the need for a new mindset in this environment.

A prerequisite for succeeding in the Social Media Sales Revolution is to set aside what you ultimately want (making a sale) and focus on what your market wants (useful information). This means that as you consider what information you are going to distribute, you must recognize the difference between content that is interesting to you and content that is interesting to the people you wish to do business with.

Examples of low-value content—the kind that will turn off your potential buyers—include

- Information about your company and what your company does
- Special pricing on products and services that your company offers
- New product releases
- News releases and updates about your business

Notice a common theme here? All these are examples of the old push-marketing kind. The motivation in sharing this information begins and ends with generating publicity for you, and therefore it has little to no value to those that you wish to do business with. Such ham-handed sales pitches collectively meet the definition of "spam" to your audience. Content of this nature will be promptly deleted, and you will find yourself being ignored. In other words, nobody is going to follow you because she wants you to sell her something. The litmus test for every online item you consider for distribution is therefore this: "Is this something that those in my online community will find worthwhile reading?" If you follow this one mantra, your online community will always look forward to reading your posts each and every time one of them appears in the in-box.

# Delivering Value-Based Content: The Mechanics

At the time that we are writing this book, we find that most salespeople we work with have little knowledge of social media other than perhaps a rudimentary presence on Facebook or LinkedIn.

If you are in the minority that is beyond that point, congratu-lations! You may find some of the following information to be basic, and we suggest that you skip over it if you wish. For the rest of you, before we get into the "how to," we will take a moment to address the "what." That calls for a definitions of feed readers and RSS (Really Simple Syndication).

## Feed Readers

A feed reader (also known as an RSS reader or an aggregator) is a software program that gathers information from websites that you have preselected and summarizes new content as it is released in a single online location for you to review. In other words, when you find a content source—whether it be a blogger, a company website, or a news source—that you want to receive updates from, if you select that site for your list, your feed reader will bring you all future updates from that source. This is the key efficiency tool in your role as a value generator, because it eliminates the need for you to conduct Web searches for content. It vastly reduces the amount of time required for you to become an online content delivery source to your community.

Some of the most popular readers available through your Web browser are Google Reader, Bloglines, and NetVibes. Since you are probably using Google already, we will use this one as an example.

To use Google Reader, the first thing that you will need to do, if you have not already done so, is set up an e-mail account with Google (Gmail). (Even if you already have a Gmail account, we recommend that you create a second, separate one for the sole pur-pose of receiving content.) After creating your Gmail account, you will see a link for "Reader" in the upper left-hand corner of your Google home page. Click on this link. Once you are on Google Reader, watch the video tutorial and you will be on your way. At this point, you are ready to begin searching for content.

## Choosing Resources for Content

You can begin finding useful information for your online community simply by searching for content sources that your followers will find interesting. When you type in keywords of topics on which you wish to begin gathering content, you will be presented with a list of online resources containing content relevant to these topics. As you review them, there are two primary methods for receiving ongoing content from them, or "following" them, to get information that is relevant to your needs. The first is the orange RSS feed icon 🔊, which usually appears on the first page of relevant content. When you find a content source that appears to be worthy of your ongoing interest, a simple click on the RSS icon is all that is necessary; the producer of that content will now continually "feed" updates to your Gmail in-box.

One very important point needs to be mentioned here. Be very selective when it comes to choosing resources that you want to follow. You probably do not need more than five or six high-quality feeds, at most, to get all the information that you can use. If you go much beyond that number, you will quickly find that your in-box is overwhelmed. You can always drop resources that aren't meeting your needs and add others. Just be picky.

The second common way to follow a content producer is to follow the instructions for subscribing, that is, clicking on "follow me" or "subscribe," and most commonly a simple link. In either case, once you have completed this simple process, you will be served updates and new material from this content partner each time that new content is posted. Now you are ready to start selecting manufacturers of content for your distribution. What are your best sources?

## Bloggers

Bloggers are invaluable and critical partners in the world of value-based content delivery. Good bloggers do more than simply produce articles; they use their creativity, personal experience, and personality to write engaging, relevant material that is typically more colorful and personalized than what you will find in standard mass-media fare. The better bloggers will be available in an RSS feed, and each updated blog entry that they make will appear in summary form when it is presented as a feed item.

When evaluating blogging resources, it pays to be picky. Taking the time to select a few high-quality resources is a much better use of your time than following a lot of mediocre ones; after all, space in your Gmail in-box is valuable. Here are some key characteristics to look for when picking leading bloggers within your field of expertise:

- *Personality.* Blogging allows much greater freedom of expression than traditional media, simply because bloggers don't have bosses (in this case, editors) to contend with. Great bloggers lend their individuality freely to their content. They use a combination of humor, personal stories, and opinion to make their material entertaining to read.

- *Originality.* Some of the most effective bloggers are also the most gnarly. You are looking for individuals who show an obvious passion for the subject(s) on which they write. Individuals who write interesting commentary that challenges the status quo are always going to be worth consideration.
- *Depth of expertise.* In the business world, industry experts—speakers, authors, CEOs, and so on—carry a lot of credibility within their specialties. Any recognized authority on the subject matter that you require is a good candidate to be on your feed list, because name recognition guarantees that the material you distribute will garner attention from those that follow you.
- *Consistency.* Writing on a regular basis requires time, considerable effort, and a professional commitment to the online community. You want to follow people who have a track record of producing high-quality content regularly; obviously, these individuals are in the minority. When reviewing a blogger's posts, look at his past work and note the time that typically passes between each posting. Ideally, you want to see a pattern of postings at least once a week if you are to consider that blog as a resource for your needs.

## Industry Associations

The websites of industry trade associations are one of the best sources available to you for content that is of high interest to your vertical community. In addition to being an excellent source of information on industry trends, changes in government regulations, and technology updates, many associations regularly publish articles written by both members and outside resources, always because of a specific application or interest of their readers. When you consider that the typical trade association has only a small percentage of the businesses within its industry as paying members, with even fewer as active participants, you can easily see that this resource is a potential gold mine of fresh, cutting-edge information for the majority of your followers. Virtually every industry has a national association, and many of these also have state chapters. Do your homework, and make it a point to follow both.

*Trade Publications*

As well as trade associations, most industries are served by a variety of trade publications, and most of these now have both a print and an online version of their products. In addition to industry news and articles, many also carry columnists who write regularly on industry topics. Again, these feeds are a superb, highly specific source of content for your readers. As with bloggers, you will need to do some research to find columnists that produce content that is worthy of following.

# Distributing Your Content

Now that you know how to get high-quality content for distribution, how do you distribute it?

As we outlined in the previous chapters on LinkedIn, Facebook, and Twitter, you have various ways of distributing your content through these social networking platforms.

- On LinkedIn, you can post status updates on your profile, post links to information and start discussion threads in LinkedIn Groups, and add content to your LinkedIn Company Page, among other places where you can share content with your LinkedIn Connections.
- On Facebook, you can post the information on your wall and your Facebook fan page. You can share the information on Facebook Groups, and you can even use the information on a landing page for your Facebook Ads.
- On Twitter, you'll be tweeting the information to your followers and anyone who is doing searches based on keywords that are in your tweets. You can also post information in your expanded Twellow profile.

But here's something that very few salespeople do, and the return is huge: create a newsletter.

## Newsletters

Before you panic, it's important that you know that putting a newsletter together is not that hard. You can sign up for a service like Constant Contact or iContact, and for a very small monthly fee, you can have a very high-quality newsletter sent out to as many people as you like. These services provide templates that are customizable even by nontechies. We know because we use them ourselves. If you're sending out a biweekly or monthly newsletter, you're doing something that almost no salespeople do. You're contacting your prospects, clients, and referral partners in a non-stalker-like manner. You're gaining credibility in these people's eyes because you're going above and beyond what most people will do. They probably think that you're putting a lot of time and effort into your newsletters, whereas in reality, you're not. You're copying and pasting all this great content, adding a few words, and there you go.

This brings up a very important point: if you're participating in the social media revolution, one of your most valuable assets is your e-mail list. You should be getting the e-mail addresses of everyone you meet. You should be adding those addresses to your database and importing that database into your newsletter list on a weekly basis. You always want to ask the person if it's okay to add her to your newsletter list, however. You can't just add people to your newsletter list without asking them. Let them know that you send out a newsletter that's not "salesy" in nature, is quick to read, and is full of content that is relevant to their business, then ask them if they're okay with your adding them to your newsletter list. Most people will agree to be on your list. Don't forget that you can export the contact information, including the e-mail addresses, of all your 1st [Degree] Connections on LinkedIn. When you're connecting with people on Facebook and Twitter, make sure that you're also getting their e-mail addresses.

At the bottom of your newsletter, make sure that you say something like, "Please feel free to forward this newsletter to anyone whom you feel would see value in it." You never know where in the world it will go. Our own personal newsletters go out to many countries because people have forwarded them and the recipients have requested to be on our newsletter distribution list. When you use a service like Constant Contact or iContact, all the person has to do to sign up to receive your newsletter is take a few seconds to click the link at the bottom.

By steadily growing your newsletter list in addition to your efforts on LinkedIn, Facebook, and Twitter, you can communicate with and add value to a very large number of people. And, most important, you're positioning yourself as the lowest-risk, most logical choice for them to do business with and refer business to.

You're touching these people on a regular basis, you're never overtly asking them to do business with you, and you're adding value to them all the time. How much better than that can it get? Most salespeople smile and dial, and when the prospect isn't interested, they never follow up or stay in touch. That's what amateur salespeople do. The fact that you're reading this book proves that you're no amateur salesperson, so hopefully you'll realize the potential benefit of implementing a newsletter as part of your strategy. Keep in mind that the primary difference between producing a newsletter and writing a blog is that the former focuses strictly on providing newsworthy content, while the latter adds the benefit of your personal opinion and unique writing style. As potential clients gain familiarity with you through all your online efforts, you're no longer just some salesperson. You're developing a know-like-trust relationship, and in business, there is nothing more valuable than that.

## Summary

The concept of customers buying from people that they like, know, and trust is the foundation of effective relationship development. People learn to like, know, and trust those who provide value to them (in this case, in the form of high-quality content) on a consistent basis.

The technology behind social media takes "like, know, and trust" to mind-blowing proportions. It offers you the opportunity to build relationships with thousands of people that are potential buyers of your goods and services. By taking a little time to learn the mechanics of distributing content, you will be able to become a value generator to your ever-growing online community.

# CHAPTER 7

# HOW TO COMMUNICATE WITH PROSPECTS ONLINE AND OFFLINE

## Netiquette for Salespeople

Despite all the dramatic changes that the Internet is bringing to the sales profession, there is one aspect of developing new accounts that has not changed and never will. There are still only two ways for a new relationship to be initiated: either the prospect initiates contact with you or you initiate contact with the prospect. Much of this book has focused on the importance of creating an inbound marketing strategy that motivates prospects to initiate contact with you because they have come to know, like, and trust you through your role as a value generator. When this happens, think of it as *reactive marketing*, because you, as a salesperson, are reacting to contact initiated by the prospect. You are responding to an incoming inquiry from a buyer who is interested in your products and/or services. Incoming lead generation is the primary benefit of an effective social media marketing strategy; it is why you are implementing it.

Proactive marketing, on the other hand, refers to your initiating contact with prospects—what you have traditionally done through prospecting. You might think from what you've read so far that we expect you to abandon your efforts to initiate sales opportunities in this new business model—that your new job is to sit back and wait for the leads to appear. Far from it! The fact is that your social media marketing strategy provides the foundation necessary for getting excellent results from future outbound marketing efforts. You still have to reach out to future prospects, although we weren't kidding when we said that traditional prospecting is obsolete. There are some fundamental differences between traditional prospecting methods and those that can be utilized in the Social Media Sales Revolution. In this chapter, we will provide you with useful, highly effective ways to market proactively to prospects within the parameters of social media marketing. Before we get into that, though, let's review some basic protocols of online etiquette, or "netiquette."

## Be Yourself

A lot of business book authors make the mistake of writing in too dry a tone, as if they were worried that injecting any of their personality into the mix would detract from their aura of professionalism. Nobody is a consummate professional in all aspects of her life, though, so it's a mistake to feel that you have to measure up to that image at every moment in your writing, too. Doing so means that you're not being you. This is an aspect of written communication that is important—remember to be yourself. Write to others the way you talk to others. Show your personality. Be *real*. People who don't know you at first will warm up to you quickly if they get to know you in this way. You will never meet all of them in person, but they will be much more likely to follow you (and recommend you to others, which is a key to your success in building your footprint) if they find you to be a likable, genuine person through the way that you write.

There was a time when there was a very clear line of differentiation between your business life and your personal life. In a lot of ways, that line is gone. With the advent of BlackBerrys, iPhones, and every other kind of electronic leash, we are no longer disconnecting from the office when we get home, or anywhere else, for that matter. The reason we bring this up is that there was a time when you behaved in a certain way at work and another way outside of work. Unfortunately, you are only one person. Many people ask us, "How should I be on social media?" We think that's a funny question. Unless you have multiple personalities, the way you are offline is pretty much the way you're going to be online. We can't outrun our character.

Being professional and having a personality aren't mutually exclusive. You probably want to do business with people who are sincere and authentic. And guess what? So does everyone else. Always remember that you're unique—and so is everyone else. Be professional, but at the same time don't be afraid to inject some of your personality into your communications. Dealing with someone who is pleasant and non-corporate-sounding is a breath of fresh air.

## You Are Talking to People, Not Computers

The world of online communication lends itself to being impersonal, if we so choose. After all, there is an element of anonymity to online communication that tends to dehumanize the way we interact with others. We can forget at times that we are talking to other people, not other computers. This, combined with the ability to hide one's identity, causes some people to abandon traditional parameters of good behavior, particularly when they are participating in polls or forums. You see examples all the time in comments posted on a variety of websites; there are a lot of people who say things to one another on the Web that they would never say in person. People who use the cloak of anonymity to say ugly things online simply because they can remain anonymous are cowards. You do not want to be one of these people.

Rudeness in the online environment is just as inappropriate as rudeness in the real world. Remember that you are interacting with other people who have feelings similar to your own. It's important that you talk to people online as if you were talking to them in person—if you wouldn't say something to someone in person, don't say it to him in your correspondence.

## Who You Are Is What You Type

The most important attribute of online communication—something that you must be aware of at all times—is the singular power of the written word. Because you are a sales professional, in your "natural" environment as a salesperson—a face-to-face interaction with another human being—there is a myriad of factors that collectively create the overall impression that a prospect or client has of you, and therefore how you are perceived. These include how you shake hands, how you sit, your appearance, your voice, your eye contact, your hand gestures, and many other, more subtle nuances. When you are communicating online, all those interpersonal aspects of you that make you who you are have been stripped away. You need to take this into consideration, because it is a fundamentally different environment from the one you are used to. In this universe, the words that you choose online have singular, absolute power over how people perceive you. Your online persona consists entirely of what you write. Take heed, be careful, and be conservative.

## Be Accurate

One of the things that you will learn quickly about the online community, if you haven't discovered it already, is that there are people online who have way too much free time on their hands. We know this to be true, because there is a legion of users who spend copious amounts of time serving in the unpaid capacity of researching content that was posted by others, solely for the purpose of finding items that are inconsistent, inaccurate, or just plain wrong. When they find a discrepancy, they get excited by the prospect of publicly outing the offending party who posted the item. Why do they delight in doing this? Because they have an overwhelming need to be appreciated and/or noticed, we suppose. Irrespective of their motivations, it pays for you to be diligent in validating the accuracy of any claims that you make, or data that you share, about a subject, particularly one that is within your field of expertise. You can get by with an occasional mistake, but repeated inaccuracies will undermine your credibility with those who follow you in the online community. If you cannot validate a piece of information, do not present it as fact; present it as an opinion or, at the very least, as information that you obtained from another source. This will give you some protection in the event that the item turns out to be bogus. Rest assured, if it is, someone will delight in holding you accountable.

## Spelling and Grammar

Your grammatical skills, or lack thereof, are another area of communicating online that affects both your brand and your credibility as a value generator. Here again, if your sentence structure and/or spelling are not consistently accurate, the same people who scour your content for inaccuracies will also pick apart your grammatical mistakes publicly and make them, and not the value of your content, the focus of the online community's attention. Always use a spell-check tool to review your writing before you post it. Carefully read your content through a couple of times, even aloud if necessary, to ensure the clarity of your message. It is well worth the time to do some editing of what you write if the extra effort results in improving the value of the information that is being presented.

# Avoid Typing in ALL CAPITAL LETTERS

If you have ever participated in online forums, you have surely seen comments posted in this manner. You can also almost hear the person screaming as you read her posted opinions, can't you? People who do this intentionally are, in our experience, either insecure, mentally unstable, or both. Never, ever use this format for typing communication. Typing in capitals has exactly the opposite effect from what is intended: THE PERSON WHO

COMMUNICATES IN THIS MANNER IS TAKEN LESS
SERIOUSLY THAN HE WOULD HAVE BEEN HAD HE
OPTED TO TYPE IN LOWERCASE.

This rule does not just apply to your typing style; it also applies to words or phrases that you feel have a need for added emphasis. If you want to emphasize a point in your text, there are much better ways of doing so than resorting to capital letters. As an example, consider the differences between the ways in which the following sentence is typed:

It is required that we receive approval by Thursday in order to meet your deadlines.

**It is required** that we receive approval by Thursday in order to meet your deadlines.

IT IS REQUIRED that we receive approval by Thursday in order to meet your deadlines.

Note that the first two get the message across adequately, and that the second provides plenty of emphasis on the need for timely cooperation without being obnoxious about it. When the writer uses capital letters, however, the recipient's perception of the message's tone changes dramatically. In the last example, you can almost hear the person shouting—an example of overkill that is completely unnecessary, unprofessional, and even rude.

Another example of the relationship between using capitals and message tone relates to sentence structure. We're not suggesting that you have to become Shakespeare; just take into consideration how the other person may be reading your words. For example, say the following sentence out loud seven times, and each time you say it, emphasize the next word. We'll put the word that you should emphasize in caps:

I didn't say she stole the purse.

I DIDN'T say she stole the purse.

I didn't SAY she stole the purse.

I didn't say SHE stole the purse.

I didn't say she STOLE the purse.

I didn't say she stole THE purse.

I didn't say she stole the PURSE.

Now, this may be kind of an odd example, but you can see how there is really little, if any, inflection in written text. Just keep this in mind when you're writing and choose sentence structures that don't cause confusion. Be as clear as you can, and people will enjoy communicating with you.

## Avoid Racy Humor

Landy has a good friend, a fellow business owner, who each day forwards a large number of jokes and other humorous content to his distribution list, which is quite extensive. Many of these files are, to varying degrees, of the racy variety. They either are about inappropriate subject matter or contain not-safe-for-work language. He sometimes forewarns those in his distribution list of the nature of his content, so those who would be offended don't have to open the attachment. This gesture doesn't matter much, though. He's a nice guy and he means well, but you can't help but notice that the "brand" that he has established by distributing this type of content to people is harming his business. In fact, we are certain that there are potential clients who would avoid hiring him because of his propensity for distributing this type of content. We are not one of them, but we cannot speak for everyone else.

Never make assumptions about your online community's taste in humor. The problem with forwarding jokes of any kind, and particularly racy ones, is that other people may not share your sense of humor, and you never know who will find something that you send out to be stupid or, worse, offensive. You cannot win here. Some recipients might find a dirty joke that you forward to be hilarious, but they are still left with a new perception of you that you probably don't want them to have. Remember that you are building a personal brand and that everything you say and do either contributes to or detracts from that brand. There is too much potential risk to your professional reputation to forward questionable content to your online followers.

## Profanity

Imagine being at a sports bar on a Sunday afternoon with a group of friends, one of whom has his wife and adolescent son in tow. You're having a good time watching football, drinking beer (with the exception of the son, of course), eating chicken wings, and talking. During the course of the afternoon, one of those in attendance has a bit too much to drink, and toward the end of the game, he goes into a profanity-laced tirade about some topic that is dear to him. Can you picture the reaction of the mother and young son who have to be present to hear this stream of exple-tives? How unpleasant would it be to be around as the mother and son at the table react? It is hard to offend some people with humor. There are certainly plenty who will laugh at the crudest of jokes. However, public displays of profanity around children is borderline intolerable.

Profanity has the same place in online communication for business that typing in capital letters does, which is to say that it has no place whatsoever. Using foul language detracts from your personal brand. It is never necessary to use profanity in order to get your point across. At no time, and under no circumstances, should you ever use it.

## Avoid Communicating When You're Angry

As one who has successfully slimmed down and kept the weight off for several years, Landy can tell you that going to the grocery store when you are hungry is one of the biggest obstacles to suc-cessful weight management. The reason is simple: if you are hun-gry when you are shopping for food, you are much more likely to select the wrong things to eat, because your feeling at the time that you are buying food (being hungry) causes you to have a temporary lapse of judgment in your food choices. Once you eat those choices, your hunger disappears—but the high-calorie food that you consumed stays on your waistline as a reminder. The same principle applies to writing when you are angry.

One of the most significant points that you should never forget about online communication is that once you send a message to someone else, you have lost control of it forever. You cannot take it back, and you cannot control to whom your words are then distributed. Put another way, once the genie is out of the bottle, there is no getting it back in. It therefore behooves you to use good judgment when communicating online—and when you are in a heightened emotional state, especially when you are angry, is a dangerous time for communicating, because it, too, can cause a temporary lapse in judgment that can come back to haunt you. The solution? When you find yourself tempted to lash out at someone else, take a break. Give the situation a 24-hour cooling-off period before you write that e-mail or make that post. You will be astounded at how different what you write a day later will be from what you were going to write just a day earlier. To quote Doug Larson: "Wisdom is the quality that keeps you from getting into situations where you need it." You cannot make wise choices when you are angry. The only wise choice is to wait until your anger subsides before communicating.

Some folks like to take a dig at someone or play the passive-aggressive card. Don't try to be "nice with a slice." If you are even a little steamed, it's better to walk away from the keyboard, cool down, and come back later. Don't burn a bridge. In the virtual online world, what goes around comes around very quickly, and that includes jabs. Remember, a person with a sharp tongue sooner or later cuts her own throat.

## Etiquette in Forums

As noted earlier in this book, online forums and groups are a superb way for you to interact on a regular and more intimate basis with others who share similar interests; there is no better way to get the attention of prospects and customers than to actively participate in an ongoing discussion group with them.

However, because of the intimate nature of the format and the continuing dialogue associated with participation, the opportunity for bad etiquette is, of course, greatly amplified. After all, the situation here is no different from that at any social event: put a group of people with different opinions into one room, get them all talking, and sooner or later a disagreement between at least two of the participants will manifest itself. Since in an online forum this disagreement is unfolding publicly, the other participants will not be able to resist putting in their two cents' worth. This is both a blessing and a curse: controversy and disagreement are what make forum participation fun and interesting, but they also make participation an activity that can get out of control.

There are two good rules of thumb to apply when participating in forums. First, avoid voicing your opinion in a way that could be considered too aggressive. Commonly known as "flaming," this creates the same perception that typing in capital letters does: you come across as a hothead who needn't be taken seriously. Second, be very careful when you feel compelled to be critical of another person's posted comments. Since this is a public forum, negative comments that you make about another person have much more impact on that individual than they would if they were made between the two of you in a private setting. Nobody likes to feel humiliated, especially publicly—and there is always a risk of getting that reaction when you are being critical. You've heard the old saying "If you can't say something nice about someone, don't say anything at all." That is an excellent rule of thumb to follow when you are participating in groups. Here is another: "It is better for people to wonder why you didn't say anything than to wonder why you did." Meaning: if there is a risk of offending someone with a point that you feel compelled to make, it is usually a better decision to simply leave the topic alone. Let somebody else do it, instead.

## How to Approach a Prospect Online

One of the best investments that a sales professional can ever make is to purchase Dale Carnegie's classic *How to Win Friends and Influence People*. This book was written back in the 1930s, but Carnegie's timeless wisdom will never go out of style. The first two sections of the book are entitled "Fundamental Techniques in Handling People" and "Six Ways to Make People Like You." There may never have been a better primer for the salesperson ever written. You can be a black belt at product knowledge and overcoming objections, but we're betting that if you haven't developed at least some form of a know-like-trust relationship with your prospect, you're never going to get the chance to use your Bruce Lee product knowledge and objection-eliminating nunchucks.

In "Fundamental Techniques in Handling People," Carnegie lists three principles:

- Principle 1: Don't criticize, condemn, or complain.
- Principle 2: Give honest and sincere appreciation.
- Principle 3: Arouse in the other person an eager want.

In "Six Ways to Make People Like You," Carnegie lists six principles:

- Principle 1: Become genuinely interested in other people.
- Principle 2: Smile.
- Principle 3: Remember that a person's name is to that person the sweetest and most important sound in any language.
- Principle 4: Be a good listener. Encourage others to talk about themselves.
- Principle 5: Talk in terms of the other person's interests.
- Principle 6: Make the other person feel important—and do it sincerely.

In every communication with someone on a social networking platform, it will serve you very well to always keep Carnegie's principles at the forefront of your mind. Why? Because most people who are using social networking for sales purposes are using it like this: "Buy my product; buy my product; buy my product; the competition sucks; and, oh yeah, buy my product." Then they wonder why no one is buying their product. It's because they're as stimulating as a shovel to the head and they have the people skills of Hannibal Lecter.

And this is a huge advantage for you. By incorporating appropriate, effective social networking platform communication principles, you will completely differentiate yourself from the masses of other salespeople who are trying to use old school "throw enough mud on the wall and something will stick" approaches. You will be a breath of fresh air. You will be perceived as a professional and treated accordingly.

When you are initiating communication with someone on LinkedIn (or any other social networking platform), always make sure that you spell the person's name correctly. This may sound obvious, but it's amazing how many people screw this up and wonder why their initial correspondence isn't being replied to. As Carnegie said, "Remember that a person's name is to that person the sweetest and most important sound in any language." Misspelling someone's name is the equivalent of mispronouncing his name, and unlike in verbal communication, he can just stare and stare over and over again at your mistake. That's not the way to get a relationship off to a warm start. Double-check the spelling of the name, even if it's Bob.

We suggest that you indicate at the beginning of your message that you know the person is busy, and that this is why you'll be brief. Get that out in the open, and then follow through. This is not the place for *War and Peace*. Less is more. Always remember that everyone has WIIFM printed on her forehead in invisible ink. (WIIFM stands for "what's in it for me?") This is actually what Carnegie was referring to in Principle 5. Make sure that one of the first things you communicate is the value that the person will receive by reading your message.

Clearly articulate what you want to say, and then add something personal related to something that you've seen in the person's profile. Maybe it's a reference to her college or a sport that she's indicated that she has an interest in. Just be sincere. Don't come across as a schmoozer. Don't be afraid to inject some personality into your message, but, as we've said before, err on the conservative side. We've all heard people who have a serious case of corporate speak and sound like drones. Don't be one of those guys. They're about as much fun to be around as having a root canal. As we said before, being professional and having a personality aren't mutually exclusive. Ask the person if she'd be open to a brief phone conversation, or to a cup of coffee if she's in your area. The best networkers and salespeople know that they need to get the conversation offline as quickly as possible. You may initiate the relationship online, but get it to a phone or face to face as quickly as you can.

Thank the person for her time, and let her know that you're looking forward to speaking with her. If you're having the introduction facilitated by a mutual connection on LinkedIn, write a short message to that person asking him for his help in forwarding your message and thanking him for his time. Make sure that you ask him not to forward your personal request to him on to the prospect, and also ask him if he'd be willing to perhaps write something nice about you so the prospect will look forward to communicating with you. The facilitator can't modify your message to the prospect, but he can write a soft endorsement for you that will greatly increase the likelihood of the prospect's replying to your message.

As we've been using LinkedIn for many years, we've facilitated hundreds of messages. Here's a commonsense tip that may not be so commonsense to everyone. If you are doing searches on LinkedIn and you notice that some people seem to be highly connected to the people you're looking to gain access to, it makes a lot of sense to develop a relationship with the connectors. If you're going to be asking them to facilitate messages for you, wouldn't it be much better if they could write a warm endorsement of you rather than just forwarding your message with no personal introduction? Of course it would. Using a third party to vouch for you can do wonders for your prospecting.

Send the message and see what happens. If you have forwarded the message and you don't get a response in a few days, you may want to reach out to your connection and make sure that he received your message. People are busy, and not everyone has developed the habit of checking LinkedIn on a daily basis. Also, check the prospect's profile for his contact information. Many people now include their contact information in the summary section of their profile, which is visible to you.

So for every minute that you spend learning the bells and whistles of social media, spend a corresponding minute studying and polishing your interpersonal communication skills. It's hard enough to be someone that others find interesting in a face-to-face situation, so in an online format, where there is no eye contact, no vocal tone, and no pace of speech, you want to stack the deck in your favor by using impeccable communication skills. You will be a breath of fresh air and will be perceived as disarmingly authentic.

# Offline Applications for Online Marketing

The fact that you are developing relationships online does not mean that you have to limit your communication with prospects to that medium. Given that gaining an initial face-to-face meeting is usually the objective of your proactive marketing effort, there is nothing to prevent you from stepping outside of social media to initiate that dialogue with a prospective client. The key is to follow the same basic guidelines of online etiquette when communicating offline, which we will review here.

### Avoid Cold Call Approaches

When it comes to proactive marketing, one of the most beneficial aspects of a robust social media marketing effort is that there is simply no practical reason for you to have to make a cold call on a prospect to get an appointment. This is because virtually everyone that you have an interest in doing business with either "knows" you online or knows someone who does. Once your online network grows to a certain point, you will find that this is true. As we have seen, the first rule of social networking— that people like to do business with people that they like, know, and trust—trumps any cold-calling technique that ever existed, hands down.

This means that you will not be using traditional interruption-based marketing techniques (namely, telephone cold calls or, worse, unannounced drop-in visits) to get face time—a meeting with a qualified prospective buyer. Like our online marketing efforts, our offline marketing will be based on familiarity and existing relationships.

When you are initiating offline contact with people whom you have identified from social media marketing, how you approach the issue of proactive marketing is dependent upon the level of familiarity that you have with the person whom you will be contacting. All your social media marketing–based contacts will fall into one of two basic groups: people who "know" you online (on LinkedIn, these are identified as your "1st [Degree] connections") and people with whom you have a mutual connection—they do not know you, but they do know someone who does (on LinkedIn, these are identified as your "2nd [Degree] connections"). These are two completely different levels of familiarity, and they require two completely different approaches. We will examine both here.

## Initiating Contact with People Who Know You

Those contacts that currently participate in your social media community already recognize you as a value generator; earlier in this chapter, we discussed effective ways to initiate contact with them through online channels. There are times, however, when it may be more effective—or even required—for you to utilize offline methods to get your first meeting with them. Some of these reasons will typically include

- A lack of response to the online initiatives outlined previously
- An inability to make contact with the person because of spam filters or online privacy parameters that have been established
- A need to provide the person with documentation that cannot be provided in an electronic format
- The simple fact that the contact is overwhelmed with daily messages to his in-box, which causes your inquiry to be buried and/or ignored

Irrespective of the reason, there is one rule of thumb to follow when making offline contact with a social media prospect from your online community: just as you do in the online world, always send written correspondence first, and then—and only then—follow up your mailing with a phone call. There are several reasons for following this protocol:

- The person is used to getting written correspondence from you via online channels, so information received through traditional methods is not likely to be ignored.

- You avoid making a cold call—the prospect is expecting to hear from you.
- You bypass the glut of electronic messages that the person receives.
- Your offline process of initiating contact is consistent with your online one.

Remember, this is not traditional "dialing for dollars" prospecting. You are making a follow-up inquiry concerning business correspondence that you first send to the prospect.

## The Letter of Inquiry

Part of offline prospecting involves writing a letter of inquiry. Your success in this area is heavily dependent on your approach, however, so it's important that you go about it in the right way.

### How the Letter Is Packaged

In a moment, we will discuss how you should actually structure your offline letter of inquiry to get your prospect's attention. It is worth noting, however, that if the package that the letter arrives in remains unopened, the letter that you write is irrelevant—it has been a waste of your time. Therefore, it is paramount that the letter be opened and read.

Keep in mind that we are not talking about mass mailing here. These incidents of offline correspondence are to highly targeted, important prospects that you have invested a considerable amount of time and effort in getting to know, and you will be using offline correspondence with them on an occasional, one-at-a-time basis. For these reasons, the most effective way to make contact with these individuals is to use one of the carrier services—FedEx, UPS, or DHL, for example—as your means of sending the correspondence. Choose the three-day-ground option, not the overnight one; this will cut the cost of sending your message from $15 or $20 to $2 or $3. Note the date that the package will arrive at the prospect's business; this will also be the day that you will make your follow-up inquiry.

### The Follow-Up Inquiry

When you make your "warm" (as in not cold) postdelivery phone call, this is what you will say to the gatekeeper as your reason for calling:

"I am following up on business correspondence that was hand-delivered to _____ this morning, and she should be expecting my call. Is she in, please?"

When you are put through, this is what you say to your executive contact:

"_____, this is (your name). I'm the person who sent you the FedEx letter."

Your prospect will, of course, immediately know who you are; next, tell her why you are calling (in accordance with the document outlined next) and ask for an appointment. If you combine the phone call with a document like the one outlined here, you should have a high success rate in securing your initial meeting.

## Writing an Effective Letter of Inquiry

The primary reason that you will need to resort to offline correspondence from time to time is that it is so difficult to get a prospect's attention in today's business climate. We are all bombarded by information from an ever-growing list of sources. This means that your letter has only a brief moment of opportunity to get the prospect's attention.

Keep in mind that the real purpose of the letter of inquiry is to prepare the ground for your follow-up phone call. Nobody is going to pore over your letter, study the contents, pick up the telephone, and call you back. This is neither good nor bad; it is simply the reality that you face. Your goal in writing the letter of inquiry is simple: you want the prospect to look the document over, get the main idea, and be receptive when you call him. That's it.

Here are five keys to writing an effective letter.

*Keep the Length to One Page*

The first thing that your contact will do when she opens the package and pulls out your letter is determine whether it is going to take her too long to read. She will look at the bottom, to see both whom it is from and where it ends, and then at the top, to see how she is addressed. Then, if she is satisfied with the short amount of time required, she will begin reading. For this reason, always keep your letter of inquiry to one page. When your contact sees that it will not take long to review, she will give you her undivided attention for a few moments.

## Have a Strong Opening

This is a no-brainer. Keep in mind that the person follows you online. Remind him that he is in your online community. Thank him for his participation there, and remind him that you regularly send him content, which you trust he has found valuable. State your business and get to the point quickly. Be specific. You want a face-to-face meeting, and the key to getting it, of course, is to explain *why* you want it.

## Highlight the Benefits

Your success here hinges on one key issue: addressing the prospect's "what's in it for me?" Your reasons for wanting to have a meeting are the centerpiece of the request. "I would like to introduce myself in person and tell you about our company" is a waste of the person's time and will get your letter a quick trip to the wastebasket. Be creative, and be specific. Bullet and bold the value-based reasons for requesting the meeting. Make it clear that taking the time to meet with you will be a worthwhile investment of the prospect's day.

## Ask Her to Be Expecting Your Call

In most cases, you be calling on the afternoon that the package is delivered. This is a professional touch that lets the prospect know you are serious. We suggest 5:00 p.m. for two reasons: most gatekeepers leave at that time, so you may have unfettered access to your prospect, and the day is less hectic for your prospect at the close of business, which improves your chances of getting her attention without interruption. You are surely aware that a disproportionate number of top executives started in sales; it is therefore not uncommon for prospects to pencil you into their schedule just to see if you actually follow up.

## Close with a Politely Assumptive Ending

"Thank you in advance for taking a few moments to talk with me this afternoon. I look forward to speaking with you then." Don't be shy about this. You have stood out from the crowd, and you have provided value for an extended period of time. You have worked hard to get the prospect's attention, and you are entitled to expect his cooperation. In most cases, you will get it.

So, what does the finished product look like? Here is an example.

LETTER OF INQUIRY

(Date)

Ms. Jane Doe, Director of Food and Beverage
Doe Dining Concepts Incorporated
(Address)
(City) (State) (Zip)

Dear Ms. Doe:

First of all, thank you for being a part of my online community. I enjoy providing content to you and my other contacts, and I trust that you have found the information that I have provided to be valuable to you and your business. I will continue to provide useful information on topics of interest to the restaurant industry.

The reason that I am writing you is to request the courtesy of a half-hour meeting to discuss your firm's current use of frozen seafood entrees in your menu offerings. Based on my past experience with multiunit restaurant chains of a size similar to yours, it is very likely that we can provide your company with several benefits that would make a meeting on this topic a worthwhile investment of your time. These benefits include

- Reduced operating costs through on-demand, online ordering for all your locations
- Reduced on-site inventory requirements for your store managers
- More menu choices, with expanded seasonal species selections
- Dependable, high-quality product at competitive prices
- Improved efficiencies through dependable, consistent inventory management

As you know from my online correspondence, I have a high level of expertise in this area of your business, and I am certain that you will find our discussion a worthwhile investment of your time.

I will call you this afternoon at 5:00 p.m. to discuss this area of your business in more detail. Thank you in advance for taking a few moments of your time to talk with me this afternoon. I look forward to speaking to you then.

Sincerely,

Webb Master
Social Media Sales Professional

THE SOCIAL MEDIA SALES REVOLUTION

# Initiating Contact with People Who Don't Know You

As was previously noted, all the people with whom you initiate contact will either know you or know someone who knows you. People who are not in your online community, but who know some of those who are, cannot be approached with the level of familiarity that you used with the first group. You will see these individuals as potential connections on LinkedIn, but the two of you do not know each other, so sending such a person an invitation is not an appropriate step at this point. You can, of course, request an introduction via LinkedIn's system if you are paying for that service; if you are not, you can bypass this issue altogether by initiating contact offline. The method of contacting the person offline is identical: send a letter of inquiry via one of the courier services, and follow up with a phone call.

The difference, of course, will be in the reason you give for your inquiry. You want to be able to cite your mutual contacts as a basis for writing. Exhaust all your referral efforts first. In other words, go through your LinkedIn mutual contacts and explain to them exactly what you are doing and what you need. Tell them that you are sending a letter of introduction to the prospect, and ask them for permission to mention them as a mutual contact when writing the prospect. Most people will respond in a positive way to this request.

Once you have done this, the first paragraph of the letter—your purpose in writing—is one of only two parts of the previously shown letter of inquiry structure that needs modification. (The other is the clause "as you know from my online correspondence," which should be deleted.) Here is the letter of inquiry with appropriate modifications.

LETTER OF INQUIRY

(Date)

Ms. Jane Doe, Director of Food and Beverage
Doe Dining Concepts Incorporated
(Address)
(City) (State) (Zip)

Dear Ms. Doe:

My name is Webb Master, and I serve the restaurant industry as a regional accounts manager for Top Shelf Foods, Incorporated. Two of my existing customers within the industry are _____ and _____, whom we share as mutual contacts on LinkedIn. I talked to both of them prior to initiating contact with you, and both of them encouraged me to do so.

The reason that I am writing you is to request the courtesy of a half-hour meeting to discuss your firm's current use of frozen seafood entrees in your menu offerings. Based on my past experience with multiunit restaurant chains of a size similar to yours, it is very likely that we can provide your company with several benefits that would make a meeting on this topic a worthwhile investment of your time. These benefits include

- Reduced operating costs through on-demand, online ordering for all your locations
- Reduced on-site inventory requirements for your store managers
- More menu choices with expanded seasonal species selections
- Dependable, high-quality product at competitive prices
- Improved efficiencies through dependable, consistent inventory management

I have a high level of expertise in this area of your business, and I am certain that you will find our discussion a worthwhile investment of your time.

I will call you this afternoon at 5:00 p.m. to discuss this area of your business in more detail. Thank you in advance for taking a few moments of your time to talk with me this afternoon. I look forward to speaking to you then.

Sincerely,

Webb Master
Social Media Sales Professional

## Summary

As a group, salespeople have never been known—traditionally—for being well-mannered, courteous, and respectful of other people's time. In fact, if anything, the stereotype of salespeople as brash, pushy, annoying peddlers has been just the opposite. As you have just seen, another traditional perception of selling has been turned on its ear by the advent of new technology. Such tactics are not just outdated and unproductive. Because of the power of social media networking, they are completely unnecessary.

# CHAPTER 8

# EFFECTIVE TIME MANAGEMENT

## Integrating Social Media Habits into Your Day

Given all the concepts that we have covered regarding your social media marketing plan, you might assume, understandably, that a considerable time commitment is required if you are to make this process work for you. In fact, you may think that the time commitment will be so significant that you cannot possibly integrate this new process into your already-packed schedule. If this is your perception, it is because you are looking at social media marketing through a traditional-marketing lens. Let us take a moment to change that outlook. Allow us to explain why, if managed properly, the time commitment is the best part of the process, because it is going to be minimal, easily accomplished, and, most of all, fun to do. If you think you don't have the time to succeed with the social media revolution, you are in for a surprise.

# Old Wine in a New Bottle

When we consider the fundamental activities that drive an effective social media strategy—maintaining a list of prospects, researching contact information, and collecting and distributing information to prospective clients, to name a few—it becomes evident that there is nothing new here; these are the basic tasks of proactive marketing. These activities have always been the fundamental building blocks of acquiring new clients. Yes, the methods that were used in the past are different from those that we have presented in this book, but the activities remain the same. Of course, the time that would be required to carry out all these activities in the old-school style would make doing so a near-impossibility. Think about it. You would need one person to manage databases; another person to research, print, and distribute articles and other items of interest; and another to scour the marketplace for new prospects using telephone directories and other print products. A private secretary, an intern or two, and half of your available work schedule would be an appropriate manpower requirement if you were to attempt such an undertaking. You have probably worked in a company (or may do so currently) where these activities are still being carried out in this way. If so, you already know what kind of time commitment is required to make this effort worthwhile.

# Time Management Advantages of Social Media Marketing

The incredible power of the Internet, and specifically the technological power of social media, has completely transformed this heretofore labor-intensive set of tasks into a very manageable and minimally time-consuming process that can be managed by just one person—you. Once the structure has been set up, the process takes very little time to execute, and it needn't interfere in any way with your normal selling activities. There are a number of social media marketing advantages, all driven by technology, that make this possible. The more significant ones would almost certainly include the following.

## Working Outside of Your Normal Selling Schedule

If you are like most salespeople, you must carry out your day-to-day selling activities, such as telephone work and face-to-face sales calls, within normal business hours. Social media marketing, on the other hand, has no such limitations. It is an activity with a 24/7 opportunity window. Since there are no time constraints involved, social media marketing can—and should—be managed outside of your ordinary selling time. (We are not suggesting that you take your work home with you at night, however.) We will discuss how and when to do this in more detail later in this chapter.

## Minimal Time Needed to Input, Maintain, and Store Prospect Data

You can forget about maintaining a database of prospects—with social media marketing, this process is already being done for you. To cite one example, your LinkedIn account, as you have seen, is basically an online, real-time database operating as a social media community. By updating their own profiles, the members of your LinkedIn community are doing the database maintenance work for you, and as a bonus, the system constantly suggests new prospects for you to add to your list. If you link some sites, such as LinkedIn, with your databases, such as Salesforce.com and Outlook, all your contact information will be automatically updated in real time as your connections change employers, job titles, and so on. How cool is that?

## Reduced Research Time

Practically no time is needed to research and locate information for distribution to your sphere of influence. Finding this information using traditional marketing methods would require hours of tedious, ongoing research. As we have discussed in this book, selecting a handful of high-quality resources and following them via an RSS feed eliminates the need for you to search for valuable content; it is served to you, fresh daily.

## Information Distribution Made Easy

Virtually no effort is required to distribute information to your followers. In the past, this would have involved making copies of an article, creating a cover letter, printing labels, stuffing envelopes, buying postage, and hauling a box full of mail to the post office. Now, the same result is accomplished with a click of your mouse.

# The Four Revolutionary Requirements

So one of the most revolutionary aspects of the Social Media Sales Revolution is its impact on the amount of time required to develop new contacts and new business. Want to research an account for key contacts? Sign in to LinkedIn and type in the company's name; the system will give you everything that you need to know in a matter of seconds—and tell you, for each contact, whom you mutually have in common. Want to send out a new article or item of interest to your prospects? Log in to your Gmail account; there will be a list of high-quality content, courtesy of the sites that you follow, waiting in your in-box for you to review. See something there that you want to distribute? Click on the groups within your social media network that you wish to have receive the information, and hit "send."

Done. All by yourself.

And what was the actual time investment on your part to get all this accomplished?

Let's be generous and call it 30 minutes; with a little practice, it will probably be closer to 20. Learning social media marketing is not that different from learning to ride a bicycle; once you get the hang of it, you keep getting better and better at it.

The use of social media has revolutionized the amount of time and effort required for developing new business—and in the process, it has given you the power to control your effectiveness and your destiny.

Consider the implications for your current prospecting efforts, whatever they may currently be, of what we just reviewed. Once you have joined the Social Media Sales Revolution, you will be able to scale back your current traditional-marketing activities, channel that time into your social media marketing efforts, and accomplish the following:

- Cut your marketing time commitment to a fraction of its current requirement

- Get exponentially more accomplished
- Reach exponentially more people
- Replace interruption-based marketing with value generation
- Build a personal brand
- Eliminate cold calling
- Have new customers chasing you, not the other way around
- Look forward to marketing, instead of dreading it

So, are you in? Are you ready to get started? Or are you thinking, "This sounds too good to be true—where's the catch?"

Actually, there are four of them: the four Revolution Requirements.

## Revolution Requirement 1: Active Participation

The Pareto principle, or the 80/20 rule, was discussed in Landy's most recent book, *Competitive Selling*, and it applies here as well. You know the basic premise: 20 percent of the participants in any activity produce 80 percent of the results. It absolutely applies to the online world and to those who participate in it. Irrespective of which social media platform is involved, you will always find that users within that online community fall into one of two groups: the 80 percent that represent what we refer to as the passive majority, and the 20 percent that we call the vocal minority.

The passive majority are the Internet's nameless masses, those who participate strictly as observers. They are spectators; they watch while others perform. They are, in the online sense, lazy. They log in without participating. They take what they need from the online community, and they give little to nothing in return. This is neither good nor bad; it is simply a reality about people in general that is manifested here, just as it is elsewhere in work and in life.

The vocal minority—the online participants who drive what takes place online—are the movers and shakers of social media. They are the active participants in the Social Media Sales Revolution. They are the value generators. They are the creators and distributors of content; they are the players out on the field, while the passive majority watch from the e-bleachers.

Don't be afraid to participate a lot on social networking platforms like LinkedIn, Facebook, and Twitter. Jump in, start cranking out content, start conversations, and join the party. Leave comments on people's blogs, compliment people on their ideas, and pay it forward. Somewhere over time, the profession of selling became somewhat dehumanized and commoditized. This is your chance to rehumanize it and to bring some connectedness to your prospects and business partners. You are here to help. Don't worry about getting everything perfect—there is plenty of room for trial, error, and adjustment.

If you want social media marketing to work for you, you have to make a commitment to become part of the vocal minority. You have to be on the playing field, not in the stands. You must be committed to becoming actively involved. To join the vocal minority, you have to bring to the table the two things that most people lack when it comes to implementing progressive change: you have to have a plan, which we have provided you with in this book, and (here's the part that's up to you) you have to have the motivation to execute the plan. These are the two pillars of all personal improvement, and they apply to social media as well.

## Revolution Requirement 2: Patience

Every year at the beginning of January, the annual influx of New Year's resolution exercisers takes over the gym at the local health club. It always becomes difficult to get on the weight-lifting machines and use the cardio equipment around this time of year; depending on the time of day, lines are common, and they're long. However, in mid-January, things begin to improve. The number of people using the facility drops by at least a third over the course of two weeks. By mid-February, most of the newbies will have disappeared for good—or at least until the next New Year rolls around.

Everyone knows that regular exercise produces wonderful benefits: weight loss, improved health, and better appearance. This is why everyone and her brother shows up at the gym around New Year's Day, willing to pay the fees and invest the time required to attain those benefits. Why, then, do so many people fall off the wagon by February? Why do they fail in their efforts to make a positive lifestyle change, in this case, regular exercise? Before we answer that question, because we are entrepreneurs, we have a business idea for the health-club industry that we would like to present for consideration.

There is one device that, if it existed, would generate millions upon millions of dollars for the health-club industry. We may even invent it some day. When we do, we will call it the Magic Mirror. Here is how it will work: potential new members at health clubs will complete an initial assessment and discuss their personal fitness goals with a staff salesperson, just as they do now. However, once the preliminaries are completed, they will step in front of our Magic Mirror. The staff person at the health club, sitting at a nearby computer terminal, will then input the client's weight-loss goals into our software program, which is connected to the Magic Mirror. Suddenly, the image of the client will change. The new image—the new person standing within the mirror, staring back at the potential new member—will be what the client is going to look like when the initial phase of the fitness program is completed and the goals are reached. The staff person will say, "This is the new you when you have completed the 12-week program"—and will give the applicant a few moments to ponder what he is seeing.

Next, the staff member will extend her hand as the new client provides his credit card for membership. You see, we are going to let each potential client preview the results of his hard work before that work actually takes place. We are going to allow him to momentarily enjoy the benefits of sticking with his fitness program, without yet having done the work. Using our system, we predict that the close rate for potential new members will approach 100 percent at every club that uses our technology—and we also predict that nearly 100 percent of all new members who step in front of the Magic Mirror will stick to their exercise program and attain their goals.

Why? Because the reason that most people don't stick with an exercise program is that they give up before they see results. They cannot visualize themselves at the end of the process; they must first endure pain with no visible gain, and they lose their motivation before they get rewarded. It typically takes six weeks of consistent diet and exercise before visual results occur. When the results do come, they are often dramatic, but unfortunately a lot of people just do not have the patience, or the motivation, to wait that long to see them.

Instant gratification does not occur in exercise programs, nor does it have a place in social media marketing. In both cases, the benefits are well worth the effort, but unfortunately in both cases the participants also have to be willing to stick with their plan without seeing an immediate payoff—and therein lies the rub.

The point is this: building a brand, earning a reputation for delivering value, and gaining a following all take time. These things will happen, but they will not happen overnight. Likewise, seeing significant sales activity as a result of social media marketing will not happen in a few days or a few weeks. It will take months, or perhaps even a year, for you to start to see real results that can be deemed significant. Trust us, though: it is worth the effort. And, unlike getting in shape, there is no pain involved—only a time commitment, which we will discuss in detail shortly.

So don't treat social media the way most people treat a gym on New Year's Day: "It took me 30 years to get this out of shape, and I'm going to get back in shape in 30 days." No, you won't. The biggest mistake most people make when they start to learn about social media and what they can accomplish with it is that they overdose on it. They start spending all their time on social media activities and let other aspects of their sales activity suffer.

They sometimes justify this by thinking that if they "cram," they can make up for lost time. As we mentioned, social media is a lot like your body. The only way you'll see results is to spend small increments of time working out. Don't spend all your time on social media, because you'll just end up "sore," or at least your boss or spouse will be sore at you for spending too much time online. The better way to go is with small efforts repeated over time—that's what produces amazing results. Spend 30 minutes a day on social media activities rather than hours a day. If there were a faster way for you to produce the results you're looking for, we'd tell you. The paradox is that in some aspects of social media, fast is slow and slow is fast. You can't rush the harvest.

## Revolution Requirement 3: Discipline

Remember that point about developing a personal brand? Your brand is your online identity. The power of branding is in consistency—making multiple impressions on those who follow you. It is important for you to remember, as we discussed earlier in this book, that you develop a reputation online every bit as much as you do offline. What kind of reputation will you cultivate in the social media world? Followers associate dependability with value. They are going to be depending on you for consistent, high-quality content. As a value generator, you have an obligation to deliver.

In his landmark book *The Seven Habits of Highly Effective People*, Stephen Covey lists the skill of setting priorities—putting first things first—as one of his seven habits. If you are going to become highly effective as a social media marketer, this part of your job must become a priority—in the spirit of putting first things first, it takes precedence over other, less important tasks. Active participation has to be a habit—a daily habit, five days a week. We are talking about making it a part of your daily routine, just like taking a shower, brushing your teeth, and getting dressed for work. You see, this reflects the first "catch" of social media marketing: you cannot be a part-time player in this environment. It is an all-or-nothing proposition. If you want the benefits that come with it, you cannot be in halfway; you cannot dabble in it. Either you are continually involved or you are irrelevant. Period. That choice is yours. Go all in.

When is the best time in the day to invest a few minutes in social media marketing? We strongly recommend that your daily social media routine take place first thing in the morning. For both your authors, the workday always starts out the same way: get up, make coffee, sit down at the computer, log in, and get busy for a half-hour. Furthermore, there is a significant benefit to doing this at home, before you head to the office: you are insulated from all of the niggling day-to-day stuff that you walk into the moment you get to work. Your social media routine is best done during quiet time—and doing it first thing in the morning is simply ideal, because you are focused, you are alone, and you are uninterrupted.

This is why we, your authors, literally wake up each morning with social media. It's what we do instead of reading the newspaper; after all, we are reading "the news" online. Not the local news, of course, not sports, and not the latest gossip from Hollywood—not, at least, at this time of day. The news items that we are reading, and the activities that we are performing, build both our respective businesses and our online presence. The news that we review each weekday morning includes updates from members of our social communities, the latest posts from our favorite bloggers, and the latest articles from our media feeds—it's daily news, it's always interesting to us because we control what content we want to see, and it's just as enjoyable to read as picking up the local morning edition. Which brings us to the final, and most important, Revolution Requirement.

## Revolution Requirement 4: Have Fun

At the beginning of this book, we made the observation that social media took over how people communicate with one another on a strictly informal, social basis before the phenomenon pushed into the business world. Before it reached the selling profession, why was it so successful? Why did it become so pervasive before it became, from a sales perspective, useful? It didn't happen because it is complicated; it didn't happen because people like to do extra work; it didn't happen because people needed a different way to communicate with one another. It happened for one reason: because participating in it is fun! Fun as in catching up with long-lost friends and classmates, interacting with other people who share the same interests, reading other people's opinions on subjects that are interesting and relevant to us, and weighing in with our own opinions.

As you will quickly find, it's also fun to make new business contacts and generate new sales. That's the icing on the cake—not only are you going to enjoy doing business development work, but you are going to enjoy it so much that you are going to look forward to it, every day, when you get up in the morning. If we can just get you to take that first step—if you will take a little time to set up your profiles properly, begin building your online community, and learn the mechanics of the process—you will become a permanent member of the Social Media Sales Revolution, and you will never look back.

We become like the people we associate with. Are there certain kids that you don't want your kids hanging around with? The reason for that is that you know that the kids they spend time with will have an impact on them. What goes for kids goes for us, too, though. As a matter of fact, the phenomenon of becoming like the people we associate with never ends, no matter how old we get. So as you have fun with social media, you'll find that other folks who enjoy social media will start showing up in your life. And you'll end up teaching one another things and having a ball together. Have fun, make money, and make a difference. Now that's the way to really enjoy your sales career!

# Time Management Skills and Social Media Marketing

As we said earlier in this book, the name of the game in sales is efficiency. Most salespeople are woefully inefficient in the way they manage their time. This is because they do not manage their time at all; they let time manage them. They live a life of reacting to external stimuli. Imagine this as the problem as a line of people queued up in front of the salesperson's desk. Some of these people are customers; some are coworkers. Others are their immediate supervisors, family members, and friends. Each of these people needs some of the salesperson's day. At the beginning of the day, the first person in line approaches the salesperson's desk with his hand out, wanting his portion of the salesperson's available time. She gives it to him, and he then leaves after taking the time that she has provided him. Then the next person in line approaches the salesperson's desk, and the process is repeated. And again with the third person, and the fourth, and so on. At the end of the day, the salesperson has made everyone happy—everyone but herself. She has no time left to do the things that she needs to do; in effect, she has sacrificed her own productivity needs so that other people could be productive. That's a noble concept, but it is no way to be successful as a salesperson. If you are going to be successful in social media marketing—or, for that matter, in selling, period—you have to make some fundamental changes in the way you use your time.

# Keys to Effective Time Management: Three Steps

The key to being effective in managing your time—more specifically, in managing how you utilize it—is to plan your schedule in advance, do the same activities at the same time each week, and then steer requests for your time to areas of your schedule where you have set aside time for that type of activity. We will now take a look at how to do each of these steps and how each ties into your social media marketing strategy.

### Planning Your Schedule

All the activities that make up your job in the Social Media Sales Revolution can be placed into three primary categories:

- Selling activities
- Social media activities
- Administrative activities

You should determine the percentage of your time that you would like to commit to each of these three areas, ensuring that the total adds up to 100 percent. For example, a reasonable mix for a salesperson would be 60 percent of the schedule set aside for selling, 15 percent for social media, and 25 percent for administrative. Keep in mind that this is only an example; every salesperson's needs are different. Allocate your time in a manner that is reasonable and workable for you. Keep in mind that 10 percent of your workweek is approximately four hours of time.

*Selling Activities*

Selling activities consist of any tasks that you perform in the generation of new revenue. This include alls the steps in your sales cycle with prospects and customers; a typical list would include

- Initial meetings with prospects
- Development of proposals
- Presentation meetings with prospects and clients
- Closings
- Upselling activities with existing clients
- Drive time to and from selling opportunities
  Time needed for selling activities: _____ %

*Social Media Marketing Activities*

We can divide social media marketing activities into daily and weekly activities. Daily activities, as we have discussed, will include

- Logging on to LinkedIn, posting updates, and checking the "People You May Know" section for new contacts to add to your network
- Sending invitations to new contacts as needed
- Doing the same on your business Facebook page

- Sending a tweet on Twitter, as appropriate
- Reviewing the content that was delivered to your Gmail account via RSS feeds
- Sending selected content to your online community via ping.com

Once-a-week activities (we recommend setting aside one afternoon per week for this—Friday is usually a good choice) will include

- Writing a new post to your blog, if you choose to write your own blog
- Sending up to five FedEx letters to prospects generated through your social media activity

Time needed for social media marketing: _____ %

### Administrative Activities

This is a catch-all category and would include

- Paperwork
- Meetings
- Postsale paperwork
- Expense reports
- Resolution of customer problems or issues
- Collection calls for nonpayment

Time needed for administrative activities: _____ %

Once you have these totals in hand, you can arrange to do each type of activity at the same time every week with a simple exercise, as shown next.

## Your Calendar Template

Top sales producers are creatures of habit; they perform the same activities at the same time every week. They accomplish this by blocking out time on their weekly schedule for the three groups of activities based on the percentages that they wish to use, and having the self-discipline to stick to the planned schedule.

In the example cited earlier, we have set aside 60 percent of our weekly schedule for selling, 15 percent for social media marketing, and 25 percent for administrative work. This translates into roughly 24 hours for selling, 6 hours for social media marketing, and 10 hours for administration. We recommend that you go to your personal calendar at this point and block out time for each of these three activities as follows: S for selling, M for social media marketing, and A for administration. Keep in mind that each 4-hour block of time represents 10 percent of your week.

This ability to plan activities in advance is the hallmark of a well-organized salesperson; by taking this step, you now have the ability to steer those requests for your time to where the request works best for your needs, not the other way around. Let's take a look at how this works in actual practice.

## Steering Requests for Your Time

Now that you have planned in advance how you want to spend your time, you have a tremendous amount of control over when other people get your time. We know what you are thinking: "But this won't work for me; I have to deal with emergencies on a regular basis that require me to stop whatever I am doing."

Nonsense. Most of those "emergencies" are nothing of the kind; they are treated as if they are extremely urgent because you, not the person making the request, choose to treat them as such. In other words, most requests for your time are not critically time-sensitive. (Note that we said most, not all.) What is needed is another habit—one that qualifies the urgency of every request for your time before you act on it, so you can act appropriately. This brings us to the "magic question" of time management. Whenever someone asks you to do something, go to your calendar, find a period of available time based on the type of activity that the request requires, and say to the other party:

"If I can do this for you by (day/time), would that be acceptable?"

And wait for her response.

The person will say one of two things, of course: either "Yes, that will be fine" or "No, I can't wait on this; it needs to be done immediately." If you get the latter response, you have permission to drop what you are doing and act on the request, because this is a *qualified* emergency. It truly needs to be taken care of immediately. Now for the good news: that rarely happens. Most of the time, the response you get will be, "Yes, I can wait until _____." When that is the case—and it will be, most of the time—you will meet the other person's expectations. You will get the task completed and keep him happy. After all, you will be meeting an agreed-upon expectation. However, there is a "what's in it for you," as well. You will maintain control of your schedule. You will complete whatever task you were working on at the time the request was made, and you will ensure that the time that you had set aside for that particular activity is utilized as you see fit. You will be managing your schedule, not the other way around.

It is this habit—planning your schedule in advance, and then steering requests for your time into appropriate places on that schedule—that frees you up to manage your social media marketing strategy and meet your online community's expectations of you as a value generator. If you are to be an online thought leader, if you are to gain a reputation for being a dependable, active participant in social media marketing, you simply cannot allow poor time management skills to interfere with your obligations to those who follow you. You should not consider this a burden. It is something that you should have been doing anyway. The fact is that having your online community depending on you to make time for its information needs is an excellent motivator to get you to take this step. So do it. Make good time management skills a part of who you are as a sales professional.

## The Ball Is in Your Court

So, are you up for it? Do you have the motivation to get up a little earlier each day, get that cup of coffee, and log on to your computer at home? Or if you prefer, to get into the office a half-hour earlier each day and get your daily social media work done there? Can you make a daily change in your routine to get the benefits of a robust, proactive marketing kick for your selling efforts? Remember, we are not asking for a lot of time. What we are asking for—no, what we are requiring—is consistency. A bit of time, every day of the workweek. A habit that you will enjoy; a habit that will have a profound effect on your ability to develop a presence within your market or territory.

## Summary

There are some significant, intrinsic benefits from getting into a daily routine with your social media marketing:

- You will get better with practice. Over time, you will learn shortcuts to getting things done. You will become more skilled at gaining the attention of prospects. You will forward content of better and better quality.
- You will build a powerful personal brand, and you will do it more quickly. You will develop a reputation for being dependable among those who follow you online. Through simple repetition, you will stand out from the crowd of resources who deliver content to your online community.
- You will keep up with the rapid, almost daily technology changes that are occurring in this medium. You will have a competitive advantage over your peers that will widen with time, as those who ignore the Social Media Sales Revolution fall further and further behind.
- You will become a qualified expert on how to use social media effectively. You will be an authority on trends and technological changes within your industry. This will cause you to be a value-added resource on sales calls as well as online. It is worth noting that the number one complaint that customers have about salespeople is this: "Nobody keeps me up on what is new." You will become the person bringing others up to speed.

So what are you waiting for? Get on board, and take your career to the future.

# CHAPTER 9

# ADJUSTING YOUR SCHEDULE

## A Blueprint for Your Daily Routine

The philosopher Aristotle said, "We are what we repeatedly do. Excellence, therefore, is not an act, but a habit." That old Greek guy knew what he was talking about. People back in his day were probably not much different at heart from people today: our habits determine who we are. As we outlined in the previous chapter, by creating the right habits, we greatly increase the odds of our success. At this point, you recognize the importance of developing effective social media habits. This chapter will cover some of the important daily details of social media marketing activities so you can implement the skills needed to succeed in the Social Media Sales Revolution.

Let's make a few disclaimers up front. As noted earlier, we are in no way suggesting that salespeople spend an inordinate amount of time on social media to the detriment of their other sales activities. Social media are what you use for marketing; marketing is what you do to create opportunities to sell. However, using social media does not need to take over your selling life; it is simply a function of your overall business activity. For this reason, you should look at social media as a tool, just as a wrench is a tool. Let the tool accomplish what it was designed to do, and don't spend time trying to become a tool designer. In other words, you don't have to become an expert in wrenches to become a master mechanic. Learn what a wrench is designed to do, pick the right ones for the job, and use them. Know that in this technological environment, "wrench design" will frequently change, and make it a point to keep up with current updates regarding your online tools.

Be advised: we are going to cover a tremendous amount of information in this chapter—after all, it is all about details. Don't feel overwhelmed, though. When you put it into actual practice, everything that we cover here takes just a few minutes a day. As we keep repeating: the most important thing that you can do is get started. Again, as you read this chapter, be sure to be logged on to your computer, so that you can participate while following along. Then you will see for yourself how it all works. As you read through this information, realize that everyone will use these steps a little differently. Some people will make this a part of their morning routine, and some will do it in the evening as their workday is winding down. You know your schedule better than anyone else, so use the following suggestions as they best make sense for you.

## Start the Day with LinkedIn

Right after checking your e-mail in the morning, log in to your LinkedIn account. When you do this, you will see the most current status updates of your 1st [Degree] Connections. Scan this information for possible leads. This is where you will see the most recent activity of people within your network—and, most important, whom they have recently connected with. This takes just a moment; the low-hanging fruit is easy to see.

A recent enhancement to LinkedIn now separates status updates into categories, including Shares, Companies, Groups, Profiles, Recommendations, Photos, Connections, Questions & Answers, Recently Joined, Recently Connected, Application Updates, and Polls. This feature is updated in real time, and it can be a powerful source of information for the professional salesperson. When you develop the habit of checking these status updates in the morning along with your first cup of coffee, you have your finger on the pulse of what is going on in the lives of your prospects, clients, referral partners, and anyone else that you're connected to on LinkedIn.

## Reach Out

As you review this information, a general rule of thumb is to always look first for ways to show appreciation to others. You are in sales; you already know that people like to feel appreciated. Naturally, people wonder whether anyone is reading the information that they are posting on their social networking sites. As you look to see who is posting what, review the status updates (and the links associated with them) that are interesting and valuable to you, and click the "Like" button associated with each of those status updates. That act alone differentiates you from a lot of other people in your position who are using social networking sites. It lets the person who posted the update know that you are interested in him and in what he has to say.

Very few people take the time to sincerely compliment people, and that's a shame, because more than anything else, the people that you interact with want to feel valued and appreciated by others. It is important to note that we are not talking here about an insincere, manipulative method of trying to get into your prospect's good graces. People aren't stupid; they can see a ham-handed sales pitch coming from a mile away. This is about building rapport, which is something that professional salespeople have always known leads to fruitful relationships. Building these kinds of connections gives you the opportunity to be in the right place at the right time when your prospect is ready to make a buying decision.

## LinkedIn Updates—a Glossary

When people modify their profiles or post on LinkedIn, these are called updates. Here's a glossary of the kinds of things you might find:

- **Companies** updates provide you with an up-to-date understanding of what is important to the people whom you are connected to.
- Likewise, by looking through **Applications Updates**, you can see who has changed her reading list and where people are traveling to, among many other things.
- In **Answers** updates, LinkedIn shows you questions that people are asking along with the answers that your connections are providing.

- **Groups** updates provides you with the opportunity to see which groups your connections are joining, as well as which new groups you may have an interest in.
- **Connections** updates will reveal to you how people are networking and whom they are connecting to. This can be a rich source of new prospects.
- **Photos** updates shows you who has changed his profile picture. You are curious, aren't you? If he looks good, let him know. Everyone loves a compliment.
- Finally, in **Application Updates**, you can see which companies are posting job openings. This information can clue you in as to which of your prospective clients, or competitors, are adding jobs—and growing.

As you can see, by taking just a few moments to look over your 1st Connections' status updates on a daily basis, you will gain a valuable insight into their interests, their activities, and many other aspects of their professional and sometimes their personal lives. This isn't about stalking; it's about keeping up with what is new, finding new opportunities to interact with your network, and looking for ways to add value.

## Updating You

As a next step, post your own status update for the day. In an ever-smaller, more intrusive, transparent, overcaffeinated, 24/7/365, Crackberry world, one of the questions that all online networkers, including professional salespeople, are asking themselves is this: "How can I keep my name in front of people in a noninvasive manner?" If you update your status update on a daily basis, you've accomplished this. When your connections log on to LinkedIn, they will see the status updates of their connections, which include you.

When you post personal status updates, take care not to post "salesy" information. Post something that you know your prospects, clients, and referral partners will see value in. By setting up your Google Alert account to point you toward new information about all the things you are interested in, you should have a never-ending stream of information that is of interest to your connections. Just copy and paste a link and add a comment like, "Here's an interesting article related to _____. I hope you see value in it, and I would welcome your comments." That's all there is to it. Just provide some good value and take the high road.

Keep in mind that by regularly posting status updates, you are also positioning yourself as a resource and a thought leader in your industry. Don't worry about having to write the articles—you will never have to unless you feel compelled to do so. There are lots of people out there who are writing tremendous content, and by getting it into your prospects' hands, you are increasing your value to them. And that's what it's all about. You're also paying it forward to the people who have written the content. Writing some of your own content is always a good investment of your time, of course, but don't think you have to become Charles Dickens or Stephen King.

Unlike on Twitter, where quantity often seems to be the name of the game, *quality* is the priority on LinkedIn. Posting one high-quality status update per day is ideal. If you have an upcoming networking meeting, trade show, or some other event that you think your connections may find interesting, post that as your status update. The important thing is to do this frequently. Remember: out of sight, out of mind. Plain and simple.

Short on ideas? You can simply post a motivational quote as your status update. When doing this, always be positive. People get enough negative feelings all day long, and they don't need to get them from you. People like to be around positive people, even if it doesn't seem that way sometimes. Adults are just kids with long, hairy legs. We still want to have fun, be appreciated, and enjoy life. Stay top of mind by being positive and providing value every day.

## Checking In with LinkedIn Groups

The next place you should go should be to your LinkedIn Groups. LinkedIn Groups are such a rich source of information that you should visit them every day. You can see what new discussion threads have started, as well as who has commented on previous discussion threads. You can also see who has recently joined the group, which is always worth reviewing. These individuals may be people whom you know, and should therefore connect with.

When you are in your groups, a great habit to get into is posting a link, a comment, or a question on a regular basis. This is a wonderful way to position yourself as a thought leader and let people know that you are being active and adding value to the discussion. Be active in your online networking and your efforts will pay off. When you post an item, you are automatically notified if someone leaves a comment, and when this happens, you have just witnessed the birth of an ongoing conversation. Voilà! You are off to the races.

Another great benefit of joining strategic LinkedIn Groups is that if you belong to a group with someone you'd like to start a relationship with, you can automatically send that person a message through LinkedIn. This would not have been the case if you had searched for this person with LinkedIn's Advanced Search and she had they come up as "out of your network," which means that she is beyond your three degrees of connections. This is hugely valuable because you have the ability to communicate with anyone who is in your LinkedIn Groups.

As you actively participate, also be aware that the advanced search capabilities are very granular. You can sort through the group members by any combination of relationship, current company, location, industry, past company, school, language, seniority level, interests, company size, and Fortune 500 status. You can also set up your desired parameters, and LinkedIn will e-mail you when someone who fits those parameters joins the group. Are you getting this? This is amazing! Never before could we even have dreamed of this type of sifting process to identify our best prospects.

Finally, once you've identified people within groups whom you are interested in, LinkedIn allows you to save those profiles in the LinkedIn Profile Organizer. With just a few clicks, you can save the person's contact information into the folder of your choice, which you have created. You can also write notes, including a message history to help you remember the relevant details about this person and any communications you've had with him. And now you have up-to-date information at your fingertips right alongside his profile. With LinkedIn's Profile Organizer, it's easy to manage the relationships that you need if you are to grow your business.

Like social media in general, LinkedIn Groups is not a place to shamelessly solicit new business. Just as a business professional wouldn't walk into a live networking event and try to sell everyone on her product or service, shameless self-promotions here are immediately frowned upon. LinkedIn Groups is a place to network, engage in discussions, learn, collaborate, and build relationships—not troll for sales.

## LinkedIn Answers

LinkedIn Answers is the next place that you should check in your daily routine. LinkedIn Answers is a database with more than two million answers submitted by LinkedIn users. There are many people and businesses posting questions on LinkedIn Answers on a daily basis because they know that experts are sifting through the questions for opportunities to show their expertise and offer help.

These are not anonymous people who are responding to questions; they're business professionals just like you. And LinkedIn users can rank the answers, giving you the chance to be seen as an expert in your field by providing the best answer. Find the field where your targeted prospects are most likely to be posting questions and start engaging in dialogue and providing answers.

As a major, added bonus from your participation here, Google indexes LinkedIn Answers, and as time goes by and you continue to participate, this makes it easier for anyone searching the Internet to determine that you can add value to him. In fact, if you so choose, LinkedIn even allows you to add the answers that you submit as part of your profile. Want to *really* participate as an expert? LinkedIn even allows you to add a widget to your LinkedIn home page so that you can subscribe to an answer category. There are 22 categories, with many subcategories that cover the majority of industries. Take a look and see if you can participate—and benefit.

## LinkedIn Events

Your next stop should be LinkedIn Events. Any LinkedIn user can promote an upcoming event, whether live or virtual. You can search by keyword, date, or location or look in "Conferences," "Tradeshows & Conventions," "Networking & Meetups," "Training & Seminars," "Fundraisers," and "Other Events." If you have some type of event coming up, you should definitely post it in LinkedIn Events. Search for the types of events that your prospects would be attending, and learn as much as you can. You can even see who has RSVP'd, so you have an indication of whether attending may be a good networking opportunity.

## Super Connectors

Probably the most important thing that you're going to do on LinkedIn on a frequent basis is use the advanced search feature. As we discussed in a previous chapter, the laserlike precision with which you can identify your ideal prospects and the ability to determine how you're connected to your ideal prospects is truly amazing. This brings up an important point. In order to use LinkedIn most effectively, one of your goals should be to get connected to as many super connectors as you can. Super connectors are people who have very large LinkedIn networks.

As you might imagine, your authors between them have millions of LinkedIn Connections and will be happy to connect with you, which in turn grows your LinkedIn Connections exponentially. Please feel free to send us a LinkedIn Connection Request and mention that you've read our book. Yes, we can help you—but you have to make the effort.

A good place to start connecting with super connectors is to join LinkedIn Groups that attract these types of networkers. Some of these groups are TopLinked.com, LION500.com (LinkedIn Open Networkers), and OpenNetworker.com. When you join these groups, look for people who are looking to add connections to their networks. Make sure that you connect with the people with the most connections.

Remember that people tend to connect with people that they work with. By connecting with people who work for the companies with which you're looking to do business, you greatly increase the likelihood that they are connected to the person with whom you'd like to do business. Additionally, many people's LinkedIn profiles have their e-mail address and phone number.

## Bonus LinkedIn Sales Tips

- Use the LinkedIn Advanced Search tool to find people who are typically 2nd [Degree] Connections who work for your targeted companies. More than likely, these folks are not directly involved with your sales deals. Ask these people for an informal interview and determine which types of initiatives are important at their company; this may help you figure out which kinds of buying processes are used at that company. Be authentic and transparent. Help people and build your network of "internal champions."

- Send LinkedIn Invitations to everyone with whom you meet, especially those with whom you network. You never know where these connections will lead. Even if these people leave the company they are working at now, their LinkedIn profile will follow them to their new company, and that will increase the number of connections you have at other companies that you may be in a position to do business with.
- Write recommendations for folks for whom you're in a position to do so. Pay it forward. Write recommendations for clients with whom you've built relationships. After they accept your recommendation, the next page that they see is a page asking them to write a recommendation for you if they're in a position to do so. And you know they are. And they're probably never going to feel better about writing a recommendation for you than they will right after they accept the glowing recommendation that you've just written for them.
- As of this writing, LinkedIn is rolling out a new feature called LinkedIn Signal. This allows you to search for tweets that LinkedIn users have sent based on keyword, geography, industry, and a number of other parameters. Leverage this tool to determine conversations that your connections are having that may be sales opportunities.
- When conducting advanced searches based on job titles, geography, and companies, also type in the name of a university that has recently won a major game. Type the name of the sport into the keyword field, and LinkedIn will show who has that keyword in their interests. Now you know the people who are most likely very happy because their alma mater won

the game. Find their contact information in their profile and call them to congratulate them. Jeez—talk about separating yourself from your competition!

- For a fee, LinkedIn provides LinkedIn Direct Ads, which allows you to target your exact audience so that its members see your event when they log on to LinkedIn. As of this writing, there are new functions coming to LinkedIn Events that LinkedIn has indicated will help its users target the market for their future events with even greater focus.

- Look at LinkedIn Jobs to see whether there are any openings at the companies that you are identifying to sell to. There may be an opportunity to refer someone for the position, or, as we've seen in the past, there may be an opportunity for you to learn who may be interested in your product or service if it enables the job poster to eliminate or outsource the position.

- You should also check your company page to see if anyone new is following your company. There must be a reason that someone new has decided to see what's happening on your company page. Remember that LinkedIn will send this person an update of any news related to your company every five days.

- Unlike connections on Facebook and Twitter, you can export your LinkedIn connections. Make sure that you export your connections to Outlook or the CRM solution that you use.

Developing the habit of logging in to your LinkedIn account on a daily basis will pay big dividends. This is where your prospects, clients, and referral partners are spending time, and you should too. Get in, use LinkedIn wisely, and get out and on with your day.

# Time for Twitter

After you're done checking your LinkedIn account, you should head over to Twitter and check out your Hootsuite account. One of the great things about this application is that while you're busy working and doing everything else in your life, Hootsuite is in the background gathering and sorting the information that's important to you.

As we covered in a previous chapter, you have set up your Hootsuite account based on information that you want to monitor via Twitter: your name, your company, your products or services, keywords related to your company, your competition, its products or services, key individuals at your competitor companies, and keywords related to people talking about things that you can assist with. That may be a mouthful, but these are the things that truly matter.

Open up your Hootsuite account and check your Home Feed in your Name tab. What are people talking about this morning? You can check as far back in time as you like, but you don't want this to become a huge investment of time, so depending on the number of people you're following, go back a few hours to scan what those folks are tweeting. This shouldn't take more than five minutes.

When you see something interesting, click on it and check it out. Is it something that you think your followers would see value and have interest in? If so, retweet it to your followers, and if you still have some of your 140 characters left, add a comment. It's always nice to say thanks to the person whom you're retweeting it from. Or, you can add a comment, knowing that your followers will be able to see whom you retweeted it from in the message anyway. Never pass up an opportunity to say thanks and show appreciation.

Next, check your Mentions column to see if anyone has used your Twitter name since the last time you checked in. If so, you should thank them. If the message with your Twitter name is something that you think your followers may find value in, you can retweet it to your followers, which gives you one more opportunity to put your Twitter name in front of your followers.

Just be careful with retweeting messages that include your Twitter name, as that could be perceived as self-serving. You don't want to come across as someone who has to let everyone know every time someone says something nice about you. That's a bit tacky.

If you don't want to retweet the message, you can always send a direct message to the person who tweeted the message with your Twitter name in it (as long as she's following you). A lot of the things that our parents told us when we were kids are still very true—like the virtue of saying "please" and "thank you," and "if you don't have something nice to say, don't say anything at all."

If someone sends out a message with your Twitter name in it, he has given you visibility to his followers, and that's worthy of a thank you. Most people don't thank the people who retweet their tweets. We think that this is a huge mistake and a way of alienating people—and potentially leaving a lot of money on the table.

The bottom line is this: every interaction, whether online or offline, is an opportunity to start or enhance a relationship. If you have people giving you compliments (in the form of retweeting your tweets), take an extra few seconds and thank them. And if it's appropriate, thank them publicly. Just be careful not to come across to your followers as someone who is an attention hound.

## No Twitter Fighting

Now, if it's an unflattering tweet that has your Twitter name in it (and we're guessing that this will almost never happen), remember that it's not what happens, but how you handle it. Nobody wins in a Twitter fight, and remember that whatever you reply will be public. The reply function on Twitter has a misleading name because when you reply, you're actually both replying to the person and sending your reply out to your followers. So if you have something private to say, make sure that you use the direct message function.

If you think you can do some damage control through an open, public conversation on Twitter, then feel free to reply to the message, but again, be careful. Otherwise, use the direct message function or take the conversation to e-mail or the phone.

## Check Your Messages

To see what's being said about you on Twitter, check your Name column. Is anyone mentioning you? If so, just as you did with the Mentions column, reply accordingly. Twitter is a conversation tool, so be sure to use good conversational skills. Ask questions, listen, and engage in meaningful dialogue. Notice that we said dialogue, not monologue. There are lots of people on

Twitter engaging in a lot of monologues, just as there are lots of salespeople engaging in lots of monologues. But the best salespeople know that sales are made as a result of a dialogue, not a monologue.

Check out the rest of the columns in your personal tab, and then also check your direct messages (in-box). Has anyone sent you a direct message? If so, reply, and do so on a timely basis. Replying in a timely fashion lets your Tweeple (your Twitter people) know that you are actively using Twitter and that you have good communication skills.

You should now search Twitter for any references to the people and companies that you are going to be interacting with today. Wouldn't it make sense to learn about these folks? Of course it would. You may even see what they're tweeting about. This will give you insight into what makes them tick.

## Information Flow

After you have checked your Home Feed tab, you should go through your other tabs and monitor what's going on with regard to whatever other information you're looking to stay on top of. This can be an extremely valuable process. It is absolutely amazing that more salespeople don't know about what can be accomplished with Twitter. But that's changing. The good news is that you have a large head start on your competition.

Great salespeople are similar to detectives. They piece together bits of information in order to construct a clear picture of a situation or opportunity. The best salespeople have an almost intuitive sense of this. After you've been selling for years and have been dealing with large numbers of people from all kinds of backgrounds and industries, you become very good at sizing up a person, situation, or opportunity very quickly.

Now when you take those intuitive sales skills and add to them the information flow that's going on in Twitter, it really turbocharges your sales chops. So conduct searches related to your day's sales activities. You may be surprised at what you uncover.

You can also use some of the analytical tools that Hootsuite provides. You can see which of your tweets are being retweeted, and how frequently, in a handy snapshot-type format. This may be information that would be interesting to you or your marketing department. If you discover that certain types of tweets that relate to specific information are popular, you know that you should be sending those out frequently.

## Twitter Etiquette

As Dale Carnegie wrote back in the 1930s, "Don't criticize, condemn, or complain." Don't post anything negative on Twitter. Don't use Twitter as a place to gripe about traffic, your sales manager, or anything else. Most people have enough going on in their own lives, and they don't want to hear someone else complaining about something.

If people are posting negative things in general (not necessarily about you or your company), that doesn't mean that you have to take the bait and get sucked into a negative conversation. Always take the high road and keep it positive. As people are checking out your Twitter profile to see whether you're someone they'd like to follow, they'll be reading your previous tweets. If there's a lot of inane complaining and other nonproductive tweets, we're guessing that they're going to decide not to follow you. Wouldn't you?

You may want to post one or two positive quotes every day. This is a good habit to get into. By doing so, you'll be motivating people and positioning yourself as a fountain of positivity. We could all use a little more of that. Don't tweet out a nonstop barrage of positive quotes, though. Just sprinkle them in your tweets. A little is enough.

## Getting Maximum Value from Twitter

Most professionals check Twitter in the morning when they get into the office. So make sure that you schedule some tweets to go out between 7:15 a.m. and 9:30 a.m. The likelihood of your followers seeing your tweets at 8:30 a.m. is far greater than the likelihood of their seeing them at 2:00 a.m. Again, we're talking common sense here. We suggest that you send at least a tweet or two a day. We do not suggest that you send a nonstop stream of tweets. This is counterproductive and actually tells your followers some things about you that may shoot you in the foot. By having information going out constantly, you're sending the implied message that you're interested more in social media than in your business. Don't read too much into this statement, but take it at face value. Even if you know how to use Hootsuite effectively to schedule and send your tweets when you're not at your computer, it won't be a stretch for people to wonder how much time you're putting into using Twitter. This is a fine line, so just use common sense and tweet a handful of times per day at the most. It's your goal to increase your sales and your income, not to become a social media guru. The best folks in any field always make what they do look easy. Just send out some tweets and be natural.

You may want to tweet something like "Here's an interesting article on _____. I hope you find it interesting, and I'd like to know what you think." Then attach the link, and remember that Hootsuite allows you to shorten the link so it takes up fewer of the 140 characters that Twitter limits you to. Schedule the time that you would like to have the tweet go out, and you're good to go.

Spend some time on Twitter or Hootsuite on a daily basis. There is nowhere else in the world where so many conversations and thoughts are being posted. This is a social networking platform that is growing very quickly and is only going to become more valuable to salespeople. As of this writing, only 8 percent of Americans are on Twitter. While Twitter growth in North America was a respectable 22 percent from June 2009 to June 2010, in Europe it was 106 percent, in Asia Pacific 243 percent, and in Latin America 305 percent. Overall, North American unique visitors accounted for 27 percent of the 200 million unique visitors. And considering how valuable Twitter already is for sales professionals, it hasn't even scratched the surface of what's to come. Knowing how to navigate Twitter and find the most valuable information should be a daily habit for you.

## Facebook

Last but not least, jump onto Facebook in the morning as part of your daily routine. You can also check Facebook during the day from your smart phone. Again, Facebook is a very social platform, so a lot of what you're going to see will be about all sorts of things, like people talking about the weather, whose team is winning, and other such things. But there are diamonds in the rough. Look to see what the people whom you consider influential are posting.

When you find something interesting, hit the "Share" button, and the post will also show up on your wall. Also "Like" the post on the person whose wall you shared it from. It's a way of saying thank you and giving kudos to them. It may sound odd, but if you're sharing posts on your wall that you've taken from other people's walls without acknowledging them, those people can feel as if you're just poaching their posts. Always use good etiquette. Build and enhance relationships.

Check into your fan page and see if you have any new fans. Perhaps post something of interest for your fans. At least post a positive thought of the day. People will come back to your fan page if you're updating it and creating a community.

If you're running Facebook Ads, check in to see your analytics. Are people clicking on them? What are the demographics of the people that are clicking on them? Keep an eye on these stats and determine how your investment in Facebook Ads is paying off. You will want to adjust accordingly to make sure that you're getting the maximum bang for your buck.

Check your Facebook Groups and see if there are any new or interesting discussion threads or information being posted. Perhaps post a question or thought to initiate a discussion. That's what networking is about.

Just be careful that you don't get swept into the Facebook vortex. Facebook has a reputation for being a "time suck" for a lot of people, and it can be. The goal is to scan your Facebook account in the morning and then get on with your sales activities.

## Summary

Professionals are people who have developed habits that amateurs haven't developed. In any sales organization, when you look to see who the consistent top performers are, they're always the ones who have developed the best sales habits. For many years, there were some basic habits that which salespeople needed to develop in order to be at the top of their game.

As social networking continues to evolve and morph, the best salespeople will have to stay abreast of these changes. It's just the way the game is played in the twenty-first century. These are communication tools that salespeople of the past would have given their left arm for. By dedicating a little time in your day to monitor and participate on your social networking platforms, you separate yourself from your competition. Use these tools effectively and your sales results will soar.

# CHAPTER 10

# THE FUTURE OF SELLING

## Join the Revolution

If you have read this far, you now have the tools that you need to join the Social Media Sales Revolution. You have invested the time required to make a significant addition to your professional education. Congratulations are in order! While your brain may be flash-fried from all the information that you have absorbed, putting this process into practice is a lot easier, and involves a lot less work, than you think. At this point, however, you may be a bit intimidated; how much so will probably depend on the role that social media currently plays in both your personal and professional life. We said this before, and we will say it again here: it is not nearly as complicated as it seems. Once you start implementing the concepts that we have shown you, you are going to realize that a chimpanzee can do this stuff.

## Adapting to Change

Yes, this is a book about change. Yes, the selling profession is about to experience a profound change with regard to new business development, courtesy of social media marketing. Yes, you are going to have to change, too.

Get used to it! You are in sales. Change is a daily aspect of your life. Unlike other people, you don't do the same thing every day; for you, every day brings something different. Most of your office peers sit at a desk all day. Why is this? In part, because they like the security of having a repetitive, predictable environment in which to work. There is nothing wrong with that; it is just not for you. In fact, we know that you would go absolutely nuts after two weeks of that, wouldn't you? Of course you would. You cannot imagine working in an environment in which everything is predictable and everything is the same. You are cut from a different cloth. You thrive on change.

Yet fear of change, in our experience, is the underlying reason why salespeople run into productivity issues during their careers. While this is hardly a problem that was created by the Internet, unwillingness to make the changes that the Internet has brought manifests itself in a myriad of ways. To cite a few examples, we still see salespeople who manage their account lists with flash cards that are alphabetically sorted in a shoe box. We still see certain sales teams scouring the Yellow Pages and print directories to find potential selling opportunities. We still go out on sales calls with reps who believe that making drop-in cold calls on prospects is the most efficient way for them to develop new sales leads. We see these things every day.

We can advise these people to adapt to the changes that social media are bringing, but we cannot force them to do so. When all is said and done, we also know that we will not need to force them to. We will let the marketplace do that for us. Eventually, external pressure exerted by the technological shifts outlined in this book will force them to change whether they want to or not. Unfortunately, by the time that those who resist these changes are forced to adapt to them, those who proactively decided, today, to embrace those changes will be far, far ahead.

How you look at social media, and how much you understand about how to use them, will determine your success in adapting to these changes. Our fellow author and speaker Denis Waitley has a great piece of advice about dealing with change: "You must welcome change as the rule, but not as your ruler." As we said previously, social media marketing is a tool in your toolbox. Yes, it is a monster of a tool, but it is a monster that you can keep on a short, manageable leash. Social media marketing isn't going to take over your selling efforts. If you embrace it, it is only going to enhance them.

## The Larval Stage

One fundamental aspect of selling that people who are not in sales do not understand is the amount of skill involved in leading a buyer successfully through the process of making a purchase decision. This doesn't involve stereotypical tricks or gimmicks; it requires concrete leadership during the steps of the buying cycle. There is neither time nor space to discuss those skills here, but the fact is that there is a whole lot more to selling than schmoozing with people and asking for business. You, and we, already know that. What you may have forgotten—what most of us forget as our careers take off and progress—is that the initial process of learning to become an effective salesperson involves a steep learning curve. After all, do you remember what your first year in sales was like? The product knowledge. The sales calls with your boss. The hard work with little to initially show for it. The way you had to answer customers' questions with "let me get back to you on that" on a daily basis. The realization that the people you called on did not take you seriously because you were new. The long climb to building a client base and your income.

Yes, you remember. That was no fun, but it was a rite of passage that every person in sales, including both us and you, had to go through when beginning a sales career. There is no getting around the fact that everyone has to earn his stripes in any career, including this one.

We always get a laugh in our speaking engagements when we refer to new salespeople as "sales larvae." It's not a term that is meant to be demeaning, but it is funny if you think about it. It conjures up an image, doesn't it? Sightless, legless, helpless little reps who eventually wriggle out of their training cocoons and mutate into full-fledged sales professionals.

This brings up the primary reason that the average salesperson never reaches her full potential: she thinks that this transformation process happens only once. In other words, once they learn how to sell, most salespeople stop working on their education. Yes, all of us do our stint as sales larvae, but high-achieving salespeople never stop mutating. They realize that there is always a remnant of the sales larva in them that needs nurturing. They already accept and manage the point that we have hammered home throughout this book: that change is constant, that there is always a better way to do something, and that, if you look for that way, you will find it. That is why they read books, to cite one example; it is also why you purchased and read this one. A common term for this habit is *continuous improvement.*

The larval stage is, at the present time, the only developmental stage that exists when it comes to social media marketing and the selling profession. The fact is that the vast majority of salespeople have only a rudimentary knowledge of social media and virtually no concept of how social media interface with their selling efforts. To illustrate: does the following list describe you with regard to your social media activity prior to having read our book?

- You had a LinkedIn account, but it was not complete; you visited it only occasionally, and you didn't do anything with it other than accept and send invitations to connect.
- You had a personal Facebook account, but you did nothing on Facebook to enhance your selling efforts.
- You knew what Twitter was, but, as we alluded to in Chapter 3, you thought it was a waste of time and did nothing with it.
- You knew what a blog was, but you did not follow any bloggers nor did you write your own blog.

Does that sound like you? Don't feel bad. When it comes to social media, the selling profession is currently infested—no, saturated—with sales larvae. Like it or not, because of the Internet, you are back to the larval stage of selling. And what an opportunity you have.

We believe without reservation that your decision to read this book at this moment in time is one of the wisest decisions that you have ever made, because it offers you the greatest opportunity to leverage new technology and new marketing skills to develop new business. You see, the Social Media Sales Revolution has just barely begun. With this book, we are officially launching that revolution. And because you made the decision to buy and read it, we can offer you a seat in the front row of the shiny new sales rocket ship that in a few short years will be carrying millions of salespeople. As with any great opportunity, the trick is to get in early, before everyone else figures out what you already know. And in this case, you can—that is, if you get off your duff, right now, and seize the opportunity that just fell into your lap. Don't delay another moment. Space in first class is extremely limited and is provided on a first-come, first-served basis. Those who loiter will end up in coach.

## Kevin's Story

This book begins with Landy relating the story of the beginning of his sales career; we will end it with the story of how Kevin began his. He used his experiences as a fledgling salesperson to establish the mindset required for adapting to new ideas, noting the many ways in which his selling career has been influenced over the years by the changes that technology had brought. Landy is a natural; he was genetically designed to be an excellent salesperson. Kevin was not; in fact, he began his working life as a highly trained professional in a completely unrelated field, and he was someone who never thought the day would come when he would find himself in a sales career. You might find it interesting to learn how he succeeded in sales, because his personal experience both paints a picture of what made him a successful sales professional and also predicts some ways in which selling is going as it relates to social media.

Long ago, Kevin was a full-time pianist in the New York City area. Obviously, this was a completely different line of work from sales. As a matter of fact, Kevin had the attitude toward sales that you frequently find among artistic types. You know the one, the "I'm an artist; I do not have to sell; I am above business" attitude. Yes, it is a bit arrogant and misguided, but hey, he was young and stupid.

After Kevin got married, he realized that he needed to earn more money, and furthermore, that he needed a steady source of income. But the only thing he really knew how to do was play the piano. There is one job that you can always get, no matter where you are in your career, and that is 100 percent commission sales. You can get the job, that is, but it's a testament to your ability if you can keep it. You know the routine: if you don't sell, they don't pay you. It is truly "eat what you kill" selling at its finest. And it is also a type of sales that most salespeople never experience. After all, most salespeople have some form of a base with commission structure; 100 percent commission sales is a different animal, and it is not for the faint of heart.

So there Kevin was. This was the early 1990s, before the Internet came along in full force. Back in those days, to see who was hiring, you used to open up the newspaper and scour the classifieds in the Help Wanted section. And you would always find job listings for commissioned salespeople. After Kevin cut his hair and bought a suit, he quickly found himself responding to one of those ads. He got a job in sales, and he was blessed to have a sales manager who gave him some candid advice during what was clearly Kevin's larval sales stage. He said, "Kev, you seem like a nice guy. Let me give you some advice. What most people do when they get into sales is they get all the Zig Ziglar, Brian Tracy, and Tom Hopkins books and learn ninja closing lines. But they miss the BFO."

Kevin asked, "What's the BFO?"

"The blinding flash of the obvious," the manager answered.

"So what's the blinding flash of the obvious?" Kevin asked.

The manager said, "The blinding flash of the obvious is that regardless of who you are or what you do for a living, your ability to communicate with and build relationships with people will always trump pure technical knowledge in any endeavor. Most people never study effective communication and interpersonal skills, and they have all the evidence to prove that they've never studied these skills. Most people figure out what they're going to do for a living, then get their head down and run full speed to get all the appropriate credentials and letters after their name, which, by the way, is just technical stuff. They miss the point that unless you are Tom Hanks living on an island somewhere with a volleyball named Wilson, you are going to be interacting with people every day, no matter what your job is. Doubly so, if you are in sales."

Kevin found this point very interesting. The manager went on to say, "Kev, get your butt down to Barnes & Noble and get a copy of Dale Carnegie's *How to Win Friends and Influence People* as fast as you can. This book was written back in the 1930s, but the wisdom in it is timeless. Don't just read the book; study the book. Menus and traffic signs are for reading; books are for studying. Read the book 10 times and let me know when you have."

Kevin did just what his manager recommended and studied that book. He underlined, wrote in the margins, and basically devoured it. And within a few years, he went from never having sold a thing in his life to being the top salesperson for the company out of more than 300 salespeople in 11 international offices. That year, the company was having its annual sales conference in Vancouver, British Columbia, for its top salespeople. When Kevin was called to the stage to accept the award for top salesperson of the year, the president of the company asked how he had gone from being a piano player to being the top salesperson in an industry that he knew nothing about, against salespeople who had been selling for this company for more than a decade in some cases. Kevin stood there on the stage and said into the microphone, "When I started here, Paul recommended that I get a book called *How to Win Friends and Influence People* and study it as if my life depended on it. I did, and I guess it worked."

In those days, Kevin was selling an intangible, high-ticket (that's code for "expensive") service to CEOs, and one day, right after closing a deal with a big-time CEO, he and the CEO were sitting in the CEO's office wrapping up the details of the sale, and the CEO leaned across his desk and said, "Kev, would you be willing to teach my salespeople to sell their prospects the way you sold me?" Kevin was shocked. The CEO might as well have asked if Kevin could sprout wings and fly, in terms of how much he was prepared for this. He responded, "Are you out of your mind? I don't even know how in the world I got you to buy, let alone how to teach your salespeople to do it." The CEO started laughing and said, "That's it right there. I love how you're disarmingly honest. Honesty is a key to massive sales success." And Kevin never forgot his words. *Disarmingly honest.*

Now, don't get us wrong—you don't have to be Gandhi or Mother Teresa. But when the CEO said that, Kevin started reflecting on his previous few years of sales success, and he could see a clear thread coming into view. He had figured out that, all things being equal, people do business with and refer business to people that they know, like, and trust.

That was the start of his speaking and training career. No one had a crystal ball back in those days, and certainly no one had ever thought of or heard of something called "social media." And here's where we're going with this story: for all the people who are thinking that social media is going to turn them into great salespeople, they're wrong. The whole "I'll just connect to everybody and his brother on LinkedIn, Facebook, and Twitter, then sit back while the clouds part and all the money falls out of heaven" line of thinking is idiotic. This is an important point. For every minute that you're spending learning the bells and whistles of the current social networking tools that you're employing in your sales arsenal, spend a corresponding minute studying inter-personal, relational, and networking skills. This is not as obvious as you might think. If it were, people wouldn't be treating social media like the world's greatest spam tool. After speaking to and training countless organizations, we can assure you that very, very, very few people have taken any time to study what are often referred to as "soft skills." And this is the most important point about where social media for salespeople are going.

## The Future

Your prospects have moved, but they have left a forwarding address. That forwarding address is found in LinkedIn,

Facebook, Twitter, and the blogs that they write. They are not in the Witness Relocation Program, although it may often feel as if they are. They are online. And now you know where, and how, to find them. Yes, they are moving targets, but by mastering the art of social media sales, you can hit them with almost 100 percent accuracy. As most salespeople are freaking out about the fact that no one answers her phone anymore and most e-mails go unreturned, you will go forward unfazed. You now know where these folks are and how to communicate with them as a value generator.

Social media will create more two-way conversations between salespeople and their prospects and customers. The old days of one-way monologues are over. Spam is done. The intrusive, "pitchy" ways of trying to gain your prospects' attention are so twentieth century—and, comparatively speaking, so ineffective. The communication floodgates have opened. This is the time to deepen and enhance relationships.

Word of mouth has always been the best form of marketing, and it always will be. LinkedIn, Facebook, and Twitter are the new word of mouth. Can you see that now? By tapping into more than a billion people's communication channels on social media platforms, you will have the greatest word-of-mouth opportunities ever created.

## Tools Will Change, but Principles Remain

Sales and marketing professionals are going to feel the pressure more than many other business professionals, but only if they are still trying to utilize old-world methods of speaking to their prospects. Realize that as a sales professional, your role will be more one of "smarketing" than either sales or marketing. The traditional lines are blurring. You're going to wear more hats, and that's going to increase your skills. You'll be like a well-trained runner who's always ready to either sprint or run a marathon as the need dictates.

Social media sites are only going to get more and more advanced. As we are writing this, video applications are popping up more on these sites. People are learning how to embed video into e-mail, so that when someone opens up your e-mail, he sees a smiling face and receives a brief video message. Smart phones are starting to use video on a regular basis. Skype has become a preferred tool for business professionals so they can have face-to-face meetings without having to be there in person.

Social media enable salespeople to become better consultative professionals. That's what the best salespeople have always been. Not hucksters. Not pitchmen. Not slick. The best salespeople have always been consultative and relational in nature. Let's just say it one last time: all things being equal, people do business with and refer business to people that they know, like, and trust. This has never been more true than it is now.

Remember that reading is for street signs and menus. You have read this book. Good for you. Now, study this book. Study it so much so that if you were on trial and had to prove that you've studied it, the members of the jury would have to deliberate for only about 30 seconds. They would have all the evidence that you are a modern sales professional because success leaves clues and evidence. Your social networking profiles are complete and robust. You initiate and engage in conversations and discussions across multiple social networking platforms. You continually identify the people and organizations with which you would like to do business with laserlike accuracy, and you are adding value to them on a consistent basis—massive, continuous value. People who follow you consider you to be a thought leader and the go-to person within your industry. You have earned this reputation. People are doing business with you and referring business to you. And your sales continue to grow. You enjoy your work, and it shows. Business is good. Selling is fun. Life is great!

Welcome to the Social Media Sales Revolution.

# CONCLUSION

It is seven o'clock in the morning—a Friday morning—and Thomas, formerly known as "Thomas the Sales Engine," is a changed man. It has been a year to the day since he became an active member of the Social Media Sales Revolution. Thomas now starts his day at seven o'clock instead of seven thirty. Like most high-achieving salespeople, Thomas is, as he was a year ago, a creature of habit. He still does the same things at the same times every week, just as he always has. But those activities have changed dramatically. Since Thomas is now a social media marketer, his "marketing work" this morning, as at this time every workday morning, is taking place on his laptop computer. Thomas is at home. He is dressed and ready for work. He is having his daily cup of coffee, and he is connected to the Internet.

Thomas is still the quintessential selling machine. He still has a work ethic that is without peer. However, Thomas has earned a new nickname. His colleagues no longer refer to him as "Thomas the Sales Engine," even though his numbers are stronger than ever. That label has been replaced; his new nickname is "Thomas the Internet Geek." Thomas takes this as a compliment; he thinks back to his skill set a year ago, and he is amused that someone with his background would ever be thought of as a computer techie. He also finds it funny that most of his peers have no idea of what he does on his computer, and few have even taken the time to ask. What Thomas's peers, as well as his superiors at his company, are well aware of, however, is that in recent months, Thomas has seen a significant jump both in the number of incoming leads that he receives and in his corresponding monthly sales figures. Thomas is experiencing a major resurgence in his sales career.

Thomas is still a planner, and he is still disciplined. As was the case a year ago, he still does the same activities at the same time each and every week. He now opens his Internet browser at the same time each morning. His 30-minute schedule today, like that on every workday morning for the past year, follows a now-routine sequence of events.

Thomas signs into his LinkedIn account and accepts two just-received invitations from people who have reached out to him online. One is an old college friend who works for a regional bank. The other gets his attention; it is a vice president at a local manufacturing firm. That company does not yet do business with Thomas, but three of the executives who work there are in Thomas's LinkedIn network—and all three have therefore been receiving regular content from Thomas's incoming RSS feeds. The contact does not mention the fact that several of Thomas's distributed articles were forwarded to her by her peers in Thomas's LinkedIn network, and this is why she has been prompted to reach out to Thomas. Not knowing this, Thomas accepts the invitation from this new follower.

Thomas then shifts his attention to the "People You May Know" section of his LinkedIn profile. As he does each morning, he reviews the list, looking for people that he wishes to add to his online community. There are three this morning. One is an executive secretary for an existing client. Thomas writes a personal message to the secretary, explaining his relationship with the company and inviting her to accept his invitation. The second is a former peer who now works in a different industry. Thomas sends him an invitation as well. The third is the CEO for a sister company of one of Thomas's clients. With a click of the mouse, Thomas sees that this CEO knows three of Thomas's existing LinkedIn contacts. Thomas sends the CEO an invitation, noting their mutual business relationships.

Next, Thomas goes to his Facebook fan page and posts an update. In this case, he uploads a picture of himself and two employees in the IT department of a client account. The picture shows Thomas at a computer terminal, going over a new application that the client has just purchased. Thomas publicly thanks the two employees for their business and their time at this recent meeting.

Thomas then leaves Facebook. He signs into his Gmail account and sees seven new items in his in-box; six are content from websites that he follows, and one is from a favorite blogger. Thomas likes the title of the blogger's new post this morning, and he takes a few moments to look over the content. Satisfied that it meets his standards for providing value, he logs into ping .com and distributes it to his followers.

Finally, Thomas sends out his daily tweet, via Twitter. In this case, he picks a motivational quote from a website he frequents for this purpose.

Finished with marketing for the day, Thomas turns off his laptop, places it in his briefcase, and heads for his car. It is now seven thirty in the morning. Time to head to the office.

At this very moment, a board meeting is taking place at one of Thomas's most sought-after prospects. This account is one of the largest users of relevant software applications in his entire territory, but for years it has been a loyal client of one of Thomas's primary competitors. What Thomas does not know is that this account has become frustrated with Thomas's competitor. Cutbacks in staff there have had a significant impact on client servicing; specifically, project deadlines that have been agreed to by the competitor are being routinely missed. At this prospective account, a decision has been reached to find a new partner in the marketplace. The meeting this morning is to discuss those other vendor options.

One of the company's programmers has been given the task of identifying viable alternatives to the existing software provider. This individual begins the meeting by submitting three vendors for consideration; Thomas's firm is one of the three options that are in play.

This programmer is one of the contacts in Thomas's social media community. So is the CIO, whom Thomas got to know in an online forum discussing software applications; Thomas sent him a LinkedIn invitation that was accepted seven months earlier, and since that time, Thomas has added three of the seven people present at this meeting to his online community. All three have been receiving value-added content from Thomas as a result of their participation, and all have a very favorable impression of Thomas. When Thomas connected with the CIO on LinkedIn, he asked the CIO what kind of initiatives were going on in his company and what kind of person would be a valuable connection for Thomas to introduce the CIO to. When he received the CIO's answer, he took a few minutes, used the LinkedIn Advanced Search function based on what the CIO had told him, identified a handful of people, and then facilitated introductions between them and the CIO. The CIO appreciated this, as did the handful of people. Thomas further enhanced his reputation in the industry as a go-to guy who understands the value of effective online and offline networking.

During the course of this meeting, the participants agree that each of the three vendors has the capabilities and technological depth needed to service their needs. However, aside from a few random, annoying cold calls, this firm has had no real contact with Thomas's two competitors. And let us not forget that people like to buy from people that they know, like, and trust.

As Thomas pulls into his employer's parking lot, his cell phone rings. The person on the other end of the line is a name that Thomas recognizes immediately, even though they have never previously spoken to each other.

It is the CIO of Thomas's prospect company. He begins the conversation by asking Thomas a question that Thomas has become used to hearing from his followers in social media.

"Thomas, when can you get out here?"

# INDEX

# ABOUT THE AUTHORS

**Landy Chase** is an internationally active speaker and trainer specializing in sales force and sales management productivity. Since founding his company in 1993, he has given more than two thousand paid presentations to corporate and association groups in more than sixty different industries, with clients all over the United States and around the world. He has a client rehire rate of more than 90 percent and has earned a reputation for delivering exceptionally high-value, practical content, skillfully blended with humor, relevant examples, and personal stories.

Chase's personal qualifications rank at the very top of sales speakers nationally and include repeat national President's Club awards as a sales professional, formal experience as a national sales trainer for a $2 billion service provider, and management experience directing the efforts of sales forces in both small business and major-account sales.

Chase is a graduate of The Citadel, The Military College of South Carolina, and earned his MBA from Xavier University. He holds the Certified Speaking Professional designation from the National Speakers Association, the highest earned level of excellence in the industry. A prolific writer, he has a sales blog on his website, www.sellingrevolution.com, that is read around the world. This is his second book; his first, *Competitive Selling*, was also published by McGraw-Hill. He can be reached at (800) 370-8026 or at www.sellingrevolution.com.

**Kevin Knebl** is the owner of Knebl Communications, LLC, a Colorado-based professional speaking and training company. Knebl speaks to, trains, and advises small, medium, and Fortune 500 companies such as State Farm, Herman Miller, Dale Carnegie, Grubb & Ellis, Quiznos, RE/MAX, Lorman, and Standard & Poor's on online and offline networking, social media, relationship building, LinkedIn, and Twitter. Knebl is a frequent guest blogger for a number of organizations. He has more than 20 years' experience in interpersonal skills training, sales, networking, and related areas of expertise.

Knebl is recognized as a LinkedIn subject matter expert and has trained hundreds of organizations and many thousands of individuals on the most effective uses of LinkedIn since 2004. He also has more Recommendations (850+) on his LinkedIn profile than anyone else in the world. Knebl can be found at www.kevinknebl.com.